Christian Parenting Survival Guide

From A to Z

Christian PARENTING SURVIVAL GUIDE

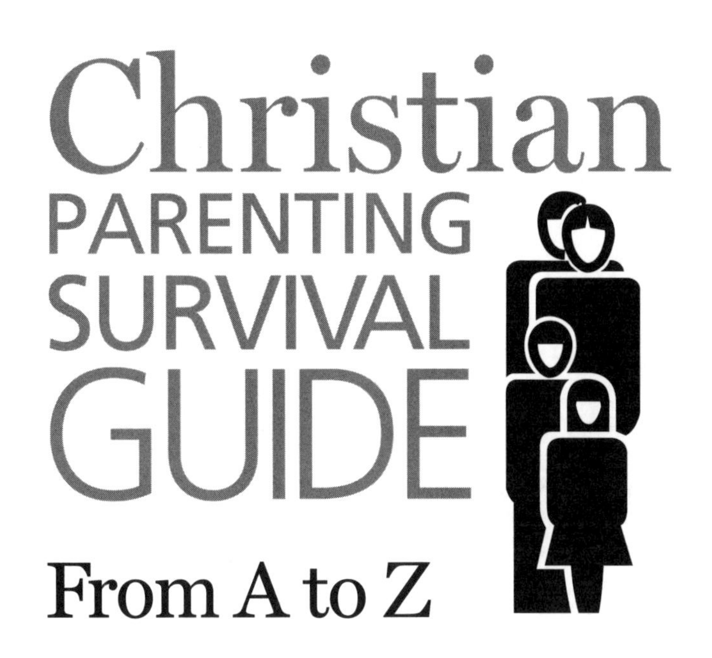

From A to Z

DAVID M. THOMAS

Twenty-Third Publications
A Division of Bayard
One Montauk Avenue, Suite 200
P.O. Box 6015
New London, CT 06320
(860) 437-3012
(800) 321-0411
www.23rdpublications.com

ISBN 978-1-58595-594-7
Library of Congress Catalog Card Number: 2006923593
Printed in the U.S.A.

Contents

Introduction

I can't imagine anything more difficult or worrisome than being a good parent. But I also know that parenting can bring deep blessings and moments of ecstatic delight. It's another one of the many paradoxes of life. If, as is said, God writes on crooked lines, nowhere is this more evident than in the lives of parents.

Parenting is a very sacred vocation, and it comes right from God. A pretty good image of God would be that of God-parent, the Almighty, Giver and Sustainer of Life. My life. Our lives. The lives of those who raise kids. Yes, God invites parents to help in the tremendous gift of creating children. We can lend a hand when a child needs a hug or a peanut butter and jelly sandwich. Our faith can be connected in a thousand ways with our life as parents. But we have to work on an awareness of the connection. We have to look hard to see the points of contact.

When we become parents, we enter an entirely new world. At times we experience side-splitting laughter, bone-chilling worry, back-breaking burdens, mind-bending challenges, and moments when we feel we're at the end of our rope. I agree with those who suggest that the world can be effectively divided between parents and non-parents. One is not better than the other, just vastly different. When parents gather for a cup of coffee or a beer, the talk quickly turns to you-know-what, or better, whose-did-what!

Recently I met an old friend for coffee. Before the waitress could even bring our cups, the question surfaced, "So how's the family?" First things first. "Fine," I responded and then gave a brief summary of the latest doings of our seven children, five of whom are now scattered around the country. "Two daughters still live with us. They are much younger. Eleventh-hour adoptions for my wife and me. Keeps us young," I added.

Our conversation, seasoned with the latest family doings, seemed ordinary, some would even say trivial. But to us, it was not that at all. It touched upon the substance of our lives. It connected with whom we each thought about before falling asleep at night. If we were worried or stressed, this often resulted from being a parent. Coffee shop talk is frequently about family. That statement is not based on hard data. It's a guess. But I'll stand by its truth.

My friend and I ordered a second cup of coffee. Our exchange moved one level deeper. We were progressing in our talk like miners who first clear away the surface materials to expose the valuable minerals below. "So how's everyone doing? And yourself? You look a little tired." Such is the world of parents.

"So how's the family?" can be a compelling and revealing personal question. Today it's also a society-wide, even global question. Political and religious leaders rightfully merge family issues into their call for a better world. And no one listens more attentively to their words than do parents.

As parents, we can painfully feel that we are living in changing and challenging times. The world of our children is not the same world we grew up in. It's even more distant from the world of our own parents. Social scientists report that the distance between generations increases with each passing year. The proof comes every time we hear music streaming out from under the bedroom doors of our daughters or sons. It's as though we are listening to sounds from another planet!

The whole of this new world (that's the scariest part) seems to have entered our homes and families. Some of it is good, but much is not. As parents of even small children, we are intensely concerned about the "bad" elements.

Many cultural forces weaken family ties, reducing their holding power and even severing precious family connections. For instance, family time has become a most precious and diminishing commodity for many. Years ago talk about the scarcity of financial resources was common. It still is. But added to the list is the shortage of time. Outsiders, jobs, the community, even churches demand our time.

What can we do? Young families especially experience this time crunch. Careers are sometimes being launched simultaneously for both the mom and dad. Employers require personal resources such as our thought processes, skills, even our muscle to produce something of value for them—not to mention a huge amount of our time.

Similar demands are made on our children's time. After school activities such as athletic practice, music lessons, school homework, and the less demanding activities like watching TV, playing computer games, and the like all extract their minutes from the day. To use the language of family authority David Elkind, our children have become much too hurried. Their parents become more harried.

Families create what various religious traditions call a community of love. Parents and their children share their time and energy with each other. The flow of life rushes between them, going in all directions. Right there, in the midst of family chaos, we can discover the Creator God. Parental love fashions the lives of children into one of life's greatest accomplishments.

What's becoming all too clear these days is that for families to survive in a sometimes unfriendly world, they need inner strength and virtue to make it. Outsiders can be encouraging and helpful, but the real work of family formation comes from inside. It is a matter of the heart joined with good common sense. And the task seems harder with each passing day.

While recently working with a local church, I was invited by the pastor to develop "a bulletin course" on Christian parenting from A to Z. Many young Catholic families were under his care. That course was an earlier version of what you are now reading. Typically, as a writer I often wondered whether anyone read what I had written. People had always taken all the available copies in the back of church, but as most church-goers know, when something free is given at church, it may often make it to the parking lot but not much farther.

Once a father came to me during the post-Mass gathering for coffee and donuts. He told me that he read each segment to his son on the telephone every Sunday afternoon. Sadly, he and his wife had divorced, and she had custody of their children. The son lived a thousand miles away, and each Sunday's A to Z created a helpful lifeline between father and son. Responses like this keep writers like myself at our computers, churning out more words.

We parents are surely tested by the demands given to us by God, the Divine Parent, whom we attempt, however imperfectly, to imitate as we contribute to making God's family a little better tomorrow than it was today. Will we survive this huge challenge? We will with God's help and some good common sense. In the reflections that follow, I hope you will find some good ideas to lift your spirit and allow God's Spirit to fill in the rest.

Acceptance

Building on firm bedrock

At that time the disciples came to Jesus and asked,
"Who is the greatest in the kingdom of heaven?"
He called a child, whom he put among them, and said,
"Truly I tell you, unless you change and become like children,
you will never enter the kingdom of heaven.
Whoever becomes humble like this child is the greatest
in the kingdom of heaven.
Whoever welcomes one such child in my name, welcomes me."
MATTHEW 18:1–5

All of seven years old, she was playing in her first soccer game. Parents lined the sidelines, each one adopting the role of coach. "Faster! Slow down! Kick it! Go, Lisa, go!" It was near the end of the game. Our daughter stood before the ball, unsure of what to do. She could have kicked it into the goal. There was an opening. Instead, she just stood there. The game ended. Some of the parent-coaches groaned. I ran onto the field. Lisa was on the verge of tears. I embraced her. Not hard, or she would be embarrassed. I told her I loved watching her play. I didn't look at the faces of the other parents. At that moment, she needed to know deep down that she was okay. There would be other games and other days. But right now, the ball was in front of me. I chose to hug the moment and my daughter. I once read it's not what you do when your children are up, but rather how you love them when they're down. So true. We slowly walked to the post-game refreshments. She handed me an orange section as she took one for herself. A squirt of sparkly juice filled the space between us as we both bit in. Holy Communion.

Our conversation about Christian parenting begins by laying down an essential foundation, which is acceptance. Like building in general, the foundation work is often the hardest. Yet it's so important when it concerns something as precious and important as the formation of a person. The foundation is laid especially during the early years. That is when children are most open, vulnerable, pliable, and easily formed. Like a parachute, their minds work best when open.

Right from the beginning—some say even in utero—children listen to and feel what's going on in their new world. They wonder about being valued and wanted. These are scary questions, especially for the very young. All of us hope a huge yes meets the child's concerns.

Our Christian faith reminds us that God's love is the reason for our existence. God accepts each of us unconditionally. This package of acceptance includes God's forgiveness. In the Lord's Prayer, we pray: Forgive us as we forgive others. Those strong and challenging words are not to be said lightly. Sometimes we find it hard to say them.

Remember Fred Rogers? His long-running TV program for small children often included him looking right into the living room of his young viewers while saying, "I like you just the way you are." Did you know that he was an ordained church minister? This was his ministry, affirming his young viewers. When asked about those words, he quickly answered something like this: "Because kids need to hear that message." Those are words of unconditional love. We all need that kind of love—parents, too, but especially our little ones. This is not a small matter. Communicating deep and abiding acceptance of our children is a message they will carry in their hearts for the rest of their lives.

We do not live in a very accepting world. Children and adults are on trial to determine whether they measure up to what is "acceptable." The story of my daughter frozen before the goal is a good example of this. Her behavior at that moment was not acceptable to the sideline coaches.

Jesus befriended many who were considered "unacceptable" during his lifetime. Samaritan women at wells, lepers living on the outskirts of town, Roman soldiers guarding the peace, people with mental problems, and one rather boisterous fisherman with an attitude. To each of them Jesus communicated acceptance. Peter, the one who seemed prone to getting it wrong most of the time, is one of my favorite examples of the accepting attitude of Jesus. While we can list many reasons why Jesus might have dumped Peter along the way, he didn't. Peter begged for forgiveness after his notorious denial of Jesus. There is no indication that Jesus struggled with forgiving him. Acceptance of Peter was abundant.

So how does this work for us parents? First of all, our accepting attitude will be tested. Guaranteed! Our love might be stretched to include our children's need for more toys and gadgets, unusual hairstyles, outlandish clothing preferences, and interest in bizarre music "sung" by strange-looking rock stars. Our acceptance of them will encompass the world of their interests, including what they just saw advertised on a recent TV program. That's not to say that we should give them all they want. Sometimes an accepting love means saying "no."

Acceptance keeps us bonded together. It helps us continue talking with each other, even though at times some of our words will have a bitter taste to them. I don't want this to sound preachy. We don't have to like the outlandish elements of youth culture. I am only saying that we love our kids by letting them know our acceptance of them!

Our accepting attitude begins with and should include ourselves. So let's take an honest look in the mirror and express gratitude for what we see there. That can be really hard! We are so deeply influenced by images of more perfect beings than we believe we are. We too are victims of advertising that can come in such non-invasive forms as an L.L. Bean catalog or even religious publications, where everyone looks happy, trim, and well dressed. Yet the person we see before us is the person we are. God fully accepts us, and likes us "just the way we are."

God's invitation to acts of acceptance is an ongoing challenge. Time has a way of changing all of us. The cute little bundle of joy cooing in the crib somehow grows into a noisy toddler, a feisty youngster, and God only knows what kind of teenager. But the person growing through these changes remains the same son or daughter.

Nowhere in the world is acceptance more necessary than in family life, where we are most recognized and known. Not being accepted in that setting can create a wound that may never heal. On the other hand, when we can sit with our family and feel an acceptance that's deep and unconditional, even crazy, well, there's nothing like it! This acceptance could be as close as we come to feeling how God is with us.

Prayer

Dear God, you have opened your arms to embrace me. Help me feel the fullness of your accepting love. May my accepting attitude be as deep as yours.

For reflection and discussion

1. How have you experienced acceptance in your own life? When and where and from whom did you feel it?
2. In what ways does our world oppose the attitude of acceptance? They say that it's a jungle out there.
3. How is acceptance a part of our life in God's kingdom?

Blessings

Counting all God's gifts

You show me the path of life.
In your presence there is fullness of joy;
in your right hand are pleasures for forevermore.
Psalm 16:11

I once heard a medical doctor say that our bodies carry enough bacteria and other destructive germs to kill us at any time. However, we have an immune system that is on duty 24/7. It fights off the killer cells and allows us to remain healthy and alive. Our bodies carry within an urge to remain healthy. And this system works even apart from our awareness. The same can be said for our beating heart, which keeps us alive even while we sleep.

Our bodies are surely an incredible creation. Thinking about this miracle gives us pause to thank God for being such an ingenious designer of our humanity. We are blessed with so much. This is always good to remember.

One night shortly after I finished graduate school, I really needed to count my blessings. I could not get to sleep. I tossed and turned as the grandfather clock chimed three in the morning. That day the mail had arrived with bad news. Our account was overdrawn. My wife and our children slept in peace while I tried to find a way to climb out of our financial hole. The monthly paycheck from the school where I taught wouldn't come for two weeks yet. The pay wasn't much because I was a new teacher. My mind kept developing plans for our financial survival. Each new one was worse than the one before.

Then the idea hit me. Think about something else. Not burdens, but blessings. I suppose I even smiled, although no one witnessed it. A line from an old song line surfaced. Something like when you're worried and can't sleep, count your blessings instead of sheep. Well, I wasn't counting sheep, only the money we didn't have. I looked at my family around me deep in slumber. Our small children were blessings in so many wonderful ways. The next thing I remembered was waking up.

Sometimes it seems God's Holy Spirit has one primary job: waking us up. Waking us not just in the morning, but making us aware of the many gifts we have been given by God, who loves us more than we can imagine. We have been given wondrous bodies that are so intricately engineered and work for us all the time. They are designed to keep us alive. Another gift is our lives. Here and now we dwell upon the earth, breathing in the riches of existence. The great religions all have morning prayers reminding us of this. Awareness of blessings arouses the feeling of gratitude. When we are washed in gratitude, we escape the pull of need.

Today we parents can think of our children in a thousand different ways. Given the reality of family expenses, we may assess their cost. The government says that it takes close to $200,000, perhaps more, to raise one child.

Here is another way to look at it. One credit card advertisement states: Soccer uniform, practice ball, cost of trophy for season's end: $122. The moment a daughter scores her first goal—priceless. It's true. The commercial is right.

A parent's life has enough stress at any time to cause arterial blockage in the heart. I know. I've had three stents inserted in my own heart to keep my life's blood flowing. My cardiologist said that

I worry too much. And whom do I worry about? Our children. It comes with the territory.

Counting blessings is not just a theoretical solution; it's needed for survival. And there's another plus. Being a grateful person changes everything. It alters how we see and what we see. For instance, try not to see a dollar sign embroidered on the backs of your children. They don't look good dressed that way. Our children come from God. They are gifts to our family and to the world. Yet too easily we can slip into the money trap. Our society is bent that way.

Have you ever heard of parent burnout? We know we have it when we look at our children with love and our first thought is that they are a huge burden. We can even become angry at them for depriving us of the joys of life we think we deserve, such as more free time, exotic vacations, a newer car. It's their fault we can't have these things. Our minds can really run with this kind of thinking. But such thoughts often go nowhere.

Parenting can be as daunting a task as anything in life. Like many parents, we carry around an up-to-date assessment of how each child is doing. We can easily list negative points about each one, describe their shortcomings, inconsistencies, failures, mistakes, and so forth. To be honest, we could assemble a similar list about anyone else, and they could do the same for us. Instead, choose not to focus on the negative. First make sure to be aware of all the positives, of the blessings that are there.

Count the blessings, every one of them. If it takes two pages or a whole book, that's what we will do. Jesus took a similar approach. When he conversed with the Samaritan woman at the well, he did not focus on her rather negative history. Instead, he looked into her heart, saw the goodness that was there, and challenged her to a better life. According to the gospel, she became one of the first to communicate the good news of Jesus to others. Would she have done that if Jesus had focused only on her life of interpersonal failures?

If a consciousness of blessings is what God invites us to, then we can begin by listing the blessings of each of our children. The more detailed our list, the better. It might be a good idea to share the list with them. In an old Peanuts cartoon, Lucy decided to start a new career by becoming a psychologist. One of the first services she offered was a complete listing of her client's faults. Charlie Brown stood next to her booth and (you guessed it) he responded with his well-known "Good grief."

The world is quite adept at pointing to our shortcomings, faults, and failures. Part of our role as parents is to accentuate the positive in our children. If we don't, who will? While we're at it, we should list our own. That's the best way to avoid the curse of burnout. Gratitude, born of an awareness of being fully blessed, is the primary immune system that keeps parents healthy.

Prayer

Dear God, you have drenched my life with your blessings. Every breath I inhale, every step I take, is your gift. Help me awaken to your generous love.

For reflection and discussion

1. Name the blessings you have experienced in the past week. Be specific and be complete. Try for a hundred.
2. How does the world approach the issue of blessings? Is our world more attuned to problems or possibilities?
3. In what ways does the church present God as a God of blessings? Or does it? Aside from the Thanksgiving Day service, when do we hear the good news of our blessedness?

Caring

Opening wide the heart

You have granted me life and steadfast love,
and your care has preserved my spirit.
Job 10:12

We turn our love for others into response and action by caring for them. Caring raises love out of its confining emotional sentimentality. It turns it in the direction of the person loved. Almost forty years ago, philosopher Milton Mayeroff wrote a classic study called *On Caring* in which he argued that to live a happy and fulfilled life requires that we become deeply caring persons. He said our growth as human persons is measured by the degree to which we truly care about others.

Unfortunately, the immense power of caring has too often been institutionalized and sometimes rendered almost paternalistic. Think of the times we say that someone is being "cared for" or "under care." We immediately think of nursing homes and hospitals and those who are unable to care for themselves any longer. We also recognize CARE as the name of the international organization that cares for the neediest of our sisters and brothers around the world. And while this kind of care is often necessary, we should not allow the idea of caring to be limited to institutional settings. We need it to touch our everyday lives, especially in family relationships. For example, my sister for many years devoted herself to caring for our elderly parents who have now passed on to the next life. Like countless others, she cared with an open heart.

Genuine caring is essentially altruistic, and it begins with determining what's needed by others. It's said that what we often do is love and care for others in ways that we would like to be loved and cared for. In other words, our care may be somewhat self-centered. So care begins with noticing and listening. Sometimes we need to ask what the other person needs.

Children can exemplify caring for others in a way that is a lesson for parents. Pope Paul VI wrote that in the Christian family the process of evangelization moves from parents to children but also from children to parents. I once conducted a retreat for parents that involved them in naming times when they learned something about caring from their children. The session lasted two hours, and as a group we filled five pages of newsprint.

One of my sons once gave me a touching example of caring. The fire engines roared down our street. This had never happened before, since we lived on a dead-end street. My wife, our small children, and I raced to see what was happening. Sure enough, we soon saw smoke curling under the eaves of a neighbor's house. A mother and her three children stood horrified at the curb. What's worse than watching your home on fire?

The expert firefighters soon doused the fire. We visited a while with the family. The damage was minimal, but with the smoke and all, it was a terribly trying time for them. The next day I met one of our sons walking out the front door of our home carrying his piggy bank. He was on his way down the street to the burned house. I asked him what he was up to. You can probably guess.

Children can often shame adults with their generosity. We too easily count the cost. They don't. I shall never forget seeing my son walking quite alone to the neighbors' home. I was allowing him the joy that comes from giving. The neighbors, of course, were touched by his gift but told him that their insurance covered the damages. Still, it was the thought that counted. His care for others still moves me years later.

The study of family dynamics often likens the family to an organic system where all the parts interconnect and influence each other. We are always observing, judging, and calculating what's good and what's not. Little gets lost. Caring actions (as well as uncaring ones) certainly speak loudly and carry immense power.

Part of genuine caring also involves concern for our own well-being. The Bible often alerts us to take care and watch out. Danger can be around the corner. We are called to love our neighbor with the same love that we show ourselves. All genuine love is connected. Taking good care of ourselves helps us care for others, especially when it's difficult, as it often is for parents.

The source of all deep care is found in God. The biblical passage at the beginning of this reflection is found in the middle of Job's lament before God. In a sense, it was a turning point for Job as he decried his woes and difficulties. Like many of us, he thought that if God truly loved him, God would not have taken away his family and possessions. We sometimes fall into a similar complaint when we begin to lose our hair, face financial strain, get colds, or lose someone dear to us. Why me, we ask. Job slowly admitted to himself that God's love and care are constant, although occasionally we humans forget. After all, none of us were there when God created all that we see around us. Mystery is always part of the answer to profound questions.

Caring can take some of the sentimentality out of love. In our world love may often be trivialized, commercialized, sanitized, and overly romanticized. Adding care to the essence of good loving helps us understand the true nature of God's love and what kind of love God asks of us parents.

Caring parents look beyond themselves to see the real needs of their children, whether they are infants, children, teens, or of any age. Care is conditioned by common sense and the perceived needs of the moment. Sometimes a caring parent will say "yes" to a child's request, and a little later will say "no" to what seems to the child as the exact same request. This can drive kids crazy.

In some ways, we have to learn how to care well, and this is one virtue that's best learned in a family. Families that genuinely care for their own will also care for others. They are magnanimous, which means they live with generous spirits. They open their hearts and hands to outsiders. Christian homes are not fortresses built to withstand the assaults of the outside world, but are welcoming places where strangers are made to feel "at home" as soon as they enter. They are places where God's kingdom has already arrived.

Prayer

Loving God, open my heart to welcome the wondrous world around me. Give me strength to care for others, especially those I sometimes fail to notice.

For reflection and discussion

1. What influences us to care for others? What most moves us to respond to needs outside ourselves? Why do some people have great difficulty in caring for others?
2. What does the attitude of caring add to ordinary family life? How do we find it there?
3. How do you feel about God's care for you? Do you think of God noticing your needs, trials, and difficulties?

DIFFICULTIES

Dealing with the inevitable

"If any want to become my followers,
let them deny themselves, take up their cross daily and follow me.
For those who want to save their life will lose it,
and those who lose their life for my sake will save it."
LUKE 9:23–24

Our world is saturated with the myth of perfection. Its attainment is promised by the countless ads we see every day. We're bound to be touched and influenced by its message, especially since we want to believe it. If only we find the right technique or product, we'll have smooth sailing for the journey. Life will be perfect.

Magazines designed for young families are overflowing with ads describing what will make them carefree, popular, healthy, and most of all, happy. We see lots of smiling faces in these ads. Parents glow with satisfaction as their children gulp down the latest breakfast cereal to hit the shelves. They want us to ask ourselves, "Why can't we be like them?"

By calling it a "myth of perfection," we are invited to examine its accuracy. Myths are supposed to be grounded in truth and reality. But is that true of the promise of a perfect life? Is there such a thing as a life without suffering and difficulties? Are there perfect families? Has anyone ever lived without a few days of darkness and gloom?

Let's be honest. We parents walk daily in a world where the spaces between us and our kids are filled with potential misunderstandings, disappointments, and conflict. Even within the same family differences exist. And wherever there are differences, there are bound to be difficulties. Because life is usually easier when we connect with its reality, let's replace "the myth of perfection" with the acceptance of some sacred imperfections as part of the territory.

Our family experienced what a misunderstanding can do. It was April Fool's Day, a day on which the value of truth is partially suspended, and people try to fool others into believing what's not true. We lived on a street next to a small flowing stream. Most of the time it was only a few inches deep, but when a powerful spring downpour came, the gurgling brook quickly became a torrential river. Our young sons loved this stream. Occasionally they'd spot a minnow or two and you'd think they had discovered Moby Dick floating by right in front of our house. In the shallow water they created sea wars involving battleships constructed of popsicle sticks and rubber bands. We parents were quite accustomed to them playing for hours in what they saw as their own private creek.

My wife and I were in the kitchen that day when we heard a cry. "Joe has fallen in the creek!" Our hearts jumped into our throats. We had seen the fury of that stream. Joe was all of five years old. We ran out the front door and down to the swollen waters that were surging past our house. "Where did he fall in? Can you see him?" we cried with desperation and panic. No sooner had we said this when his two older brothers smiled. "April Fools!" they chanted in unison and laughed. We, of course, didn't. It was not a good experience.

As I examine this terrifying moment, I reflect on how these difficult moments, and many like them, simply happen. After all, from the standpoint of our kids, this was a great way to capture the day's spirit. But they missed something crucial in their planning. They missed our side of what their idea might mean. A simple misunderstanding. There was no ill will, no attempt to hurt anyone. Nevertheless, it happened.

Sometimes family events occur outside the boundaries of logic. We mislead each other without cause. We hurt each other without intending to do so. We bring our terribly limited human tendencies to the family table. It's inevitable.

So what do we do with this truth? First, we do well to accept our condition, imperfect though it may be. Expect difficulties. Try not to be pulled down by their occurrence, and look for the blessing in each one. Jesus mentioned the daily cross and how God's wisdom often contains a paradox, for example, in losing we gain and in letting go we are gifted anew. Finally, keep caring for each other. It's healthy to admit and accept that our lives will have uninvited moments. Some will be wonderful and others won't.

At times, life can be very hard. However, that doesn't mean it's flawed, or that there's a way to escape all its challenges. Often there's a mysterious side to all this. Sometimes we have to simply trust in God's ways with us. We don't know all the reasons why our children or we their parents are not perfect.

Doesn't it seem true that in accepting difficulties and working through them, we become better persons? It helps us combat our narrow attitude. Our lives acquire a greater depth as we become more sensitive and compassionate. If our lives were a piece of cake, we could easily end up being shallow—and probably quite fat. Further, in working through difficulties, we become stronger in spirit. Like ballplayers described as "full of potential," we never know who we really are until we confront adversity. Rest is for later on. Right now we're challenged, and it's good that we are.

Can we ever speak a prayer of thanks to God for our difficulties? I'd like to think so but I must confess that on many days I find it quite difficult.

Prayer

Dear God, bring me the wisdom I need to see you in all things. Help me remain calm through days of sorrow and disappointment.

For reflection and discussion

1. How do you see difficulties as positive experiences in your life? Or do you conclude that the best we can do is just accept what comes and hope for the best?
2. How do you prepare your children for making the best out of the difficulties in their own lives?
3. What is most difficult for you right now? How might your faith and trust in God help you through the challenge?

Encouragement

Launching into unexplored space

For God has destined us not for wrath but
for obtaining salvation
through our Lord Jesus Christ, who died for us,
so that whether we are awake or asleep, we may live with him.
Therefore, encourage one another and build up each other.
1 THESSALONIANS 5:9–11

Strengthening our hearts is one of the most important tasks imaginable. From a biological perspective the heart muscle keeps blood flowing to every part of our body. If any part of the body is deprived of blood, it ceases to function. From a biblical view, the heart was thought of as the center of personal life. It was the seat of emotions, the place where thinking and judgment took place. Also, from the heart came the energy needed to love. No wonder Jesus said that where your heart is, there is your treasure.

"Encouragement" builds upon the virtue of courage. Both words come from the Latin word *cor*, the word for heart. When we encourage others, we strengthen their hearts.

Down the street from where we lived was a public school. In a quiet corner of the school the federal government of the United States operated one of the most successful educational programs ever created, Headstart. It was founded on the assumption that some children entered formal education a step behind. The playing field was uneven because regular schooling favored those without drawbacks. Headstart allowed participating children to start the race a little sooner.

Our eldest daughter was four years old. What better way to become involved in the neighborhood than to participate in Headstart? They were looking for students to help. She wanted to take part. They also favored parent involvement. The teacher was especially understanding because she was both mom and teacher. A perfect combination for kids that age.

In the class was a boy who clearly had experienced failure much too early in his life. Eyes lowered, his head always tilted toward the ground, he seemed depressed. Evidently he had already weathered tough times.

One day I went to help. On that day the teacher announced we were going to build the highest tower of blocks than had ever been constructed. The head-builder was to be—you guessed it—the boy with the sad heart.

A space was cleared for the tower. It was construction time. The boy placed the first wooden block right in the middle, then the next and the next. With each additional block carefully laid in place, the teacher turned into a cheerleader. The children and parents were led into a brisk round of applause and cheers. As the tower rose, so too did the little boy. The teacher's encouragement of him was cranked up to full speed. One by one, step by step, the person and the tower rose to the heavens. Eventually all the blocks were in place. The tower was sturdy and stood a little above the boy's head. Right at the tip of his reach. A world record, the teacher proclaimed.

The boy's eyes danced. His smile electrified the entire room. There were tears in the eyes of the parents and others of us who witnessed this miracle. Who says the creation of the world is finished? Right there Genesis was reenacted. That day wooden blocks were used to form a human person. We all saw the power that was encouragement.

There is a lesson here for parents. Maybe it's obvious but we need reminders. The complexity of parental life can confuse our approaches and dim our vision. Like a good parent, the teacher always worked at the level of specifics. She looked into the mind and heart of the little boy and asked, "What's next? What does this little guy need right now to grow as a human person?"

That's the key to good parenting. Assist our kids to the next level, one step up. That's what they need for their heart's survival.

Unfortunately, our society is very competitive, and we usually place laurels only on those who win. Instead each of us needs to be judged by what we do with what we have been given. That's true for adults as well as children.

A small segment of our society has gotten this message. One example is the wonderful program of the Special Olympics. Started by the insight and imagination of Eunice Kennedy, its philosophy and wisdom has spread to the far corners of the world. Currently, close to two million children and adults in over 150 countries are identified as Special Olympic athletes. Their goal is participation, not winning a gold medal, although if they win one, that's surely a plus.

Many of us witnessed the scene in a Special Olympics race when one of the runners fell to the ground soon after the start of the race. Instead of running to the tape, all the other runners immediately stopped, turned around, and went to help their fellow runner. Linked together, they proceeded down the track crossing the finish line as if they were one body. Surely they were of one heart, and that's what counts.

When we encourage our children, we do well to first carefully assess their possibilities and potential. We all need cheerleaders, and parents can do that task better than anyone. Children need help to move to the next step of their development. Human growth is always one step at a time. Gentle encouragement will often be the force that gets us all there.

Prayer

Dear God, help me deliver your constant encouragement to others. Inspire me to cheer for children in their effort to be all that you want of them.

For reflection and discussion

1. Note the ways in which you encourage your children. Is it something you do often or only occasionally? When have you missed an opportunity?
2. As you review your own life, who encouraged you? Were you encouraged by your parents? What effect did that have on you?
3. Do you believe that the church is an encouraging community? Can you describe times when you have felt encouraged by the church? When have you encouraged others, especially family members or friends?

FIDELITY

Investing in long-term love

O give thanks to the God of heaven,
for his steadfast love endures forever.
PSALM 136:26

Our local newspaper likes to run stories about wedding anniversaries. Often there's a picture of the couple as they look now, and next to it is a picture taken on their wedding day. Sometimes you can tell it's the same people; sometimes you have to really use your imagination. We have a wedding album with pictures from the first day of our marriage. For a good laugh, we occasionally take a look.

While the virtue of parental fidelity might seem fixed and unchanging, it really has to be flexible. After all, as marriage and family pictures show, we change. Our facial appearance undergoes hundreds of minute changes over our lifetime. We all start as babies, then grow. Our personalities undergo constant development. We learn new things, and some we forget. The story of a family is always "a moving picture."

When love includes fidelity, it flows with the changes. Marital fidelity hopefully lasts the lifetime of the marriage. Family fidelity adds the love for children that encompasses the changes that children inevitably experience. It has a "no matter what" feel to it. Love seasoned with this quality is strong love.

Faithful love is like a gyroscope that changes with new circumstances. Parental love stays steady during the times when the infant won't stop crying. It's there when the two year old learns to use the word "no" at every opportunity, when the young child "forgets" to come home after school, when the teen overspends the allotted minutes on the family cell phone, when your college student overspends the limit of the family credit card. One thing is for sure: children will challenge parental love. As the song says, "Will you still love me when I'm sixty-four?"

Okay, we've affirmed that people change, which means that true love will accept changes and keep on going. But what about love itself? Can that change too? Before answering that question, let's reflect a little on how our culture describes love.

Some persons note that our culture values immediate gratification. For proof we're given the extensive use of credit cards, the urge toward impulse buying, and the widespread presence of short-term relationships. Ours has been described as a throwaway culture. It's said that nothing lasts a lifetime. This mentality is fed by the way people move from job to job, location to location, and interest to interest. Those who want to move up the corporate ladder often have to be ready to pull up stakes at a moment's notice because the corporation needs them elsewhere. Those who fall off the corporate ladder need to be flexible. The job they want may require relocation.

In contrast to constant movement and change is the world of family fidelity. The connections are lifelong; acceptance is steady and can be presumed. It's the one community in our entire society where membership is lasting. At least, that's the hope. We all deeply desire that kind of commitment—not for a day or a year, but forever.

The demands of parenting can even exceed those of marriage. The average time a marriage lasts in our society is less than ten years. We don't have similar data concerning parenting because we can't divorce our children. Even our laws assume a lifelong relationship. At times this connection can feel burdensome. Yet many of our greatest joys in life come from being parents. We usually maintain ties with our children for as long as we live. What a wonderful accomplishment when done well.

Some of us have been present at the death of our parents. It is one of those moments unlike any other. On the other hand, some parents have been present at the death of their children. Few tragedies compare with that moment. In St. Peter's Basilica stands one of the most beautiful and most touching works of art ever created, the Pietà of Michelangelo. When Mary agreed to become the mother of Jesus, she most likely knew that she would experience great joy and deep sorrow. Just like all parents.

Parents live with the likelihood of unexpected events. We may have had to take children to a hospital emergency room, or meet with teachers or principals after "incidents" in the classroom or on the playground. Years later we may have to pick up our children at the police station, or console them after a broken engagement. The worst would be to have to identify their bodies after a fatal car accident. Such are the moments of parenting when we need to be there for our children. It's never easy. The rigors of fidelity are as intense as any other human demands. But so, too, are its blessings.

Human relationships, seasoned with fidelity, powerfully embody God's relationship with humanity. Scripture speaks of how marriage can do this. But so do other lifelong commitments, with the parenting bond being at the top of the list.

When parents gaze into their infant's crib, they don't see the road ahead. Nevertheless, it's there. What's important is that lifelong relationships are best nurtured from the earliest moments of life with gestures of love and acceptance. That's the fuel that will energize them for the long journey of their lives.

Psalm 16 speaks of God loving us with an everlasting love. Can we not say the same about the love of parents for their children?

Prayer

Dear God, we know that your love for us is constant and faithful. Help us love our children as you do, with a love that's uniquely ours, all the days of our life.

For reflection and discussion

1. What kinds of investments are you making right now in your parenting that you believe will last a lifetime?
2. Do you see fidelity as a countercultural reality? Is there anything in our culture that is assumed to last a lifetime? What do you see as undermining the virtue of fidelity?
3. Marathon runners must pace themselves for a long run. How much do you think about living for the long haul? What do you do right now to create, preserve, and protect your relationships of fidelity?

GOODNESS

Finding hidden treasure

God saw everything that he had made,
and indeed, it was very good.
And there was evening and there was morning,
the sixth day.
GENESIS 1:31

We love to make judgments, especially when it involves others. When watching the Olympic figure skating competition, most TV viewers will have their own scores in mind well before the official judging is posted. We have just painted our house, and we know that as our neighbors walk by, they judge how they feel about the color we chose. Some will like it and some will question our sanity. We attend a performance at our children's school in which one of our children is a participant. We each make an assessment of the quality of the performance. In the morning we look at ourselves in the mirror. How do we rate our appearance on a scale of 1 to 10? We can't help assessing ourselves and the performance of others. It's our nature.

My wife and I have adopted two children who had difficult early years before they came to us. We have needed the help of wise therapists and social workers. We pay special attention to their good behavior, and when we notice a positive action, we make sure to tell them. Highlight the good. That's how healing will most effectively happen. This approach is called positive reinforcement.

Sometimes parents need reminders to do this. Our judgments can be more attuned to seeing negative actions than positive ones. Sometimes the best we can say is "not too bad." Think about that phrase, which we all use. It implies that the usual condition is bad. It would be better to say "pretty good."

So how does this apply to parenting? And what's the Christian aspect? The parenting part suggests that our children often need others to point out their goodness. Our society provides rather limited indicators of goodness. By the time children are three or four, they have already taken in society's criteria for who's attractive or not. Magazines and ads feature "cute" kids. They look the right size, sport the latest hairstyles for little ones, have great clothes, and exude sparkling personalities. Our own children look at these kids and compare their own personal inadequacies and shortcomings. At three!

We know that this tendency toward negative judgments is not limited to the young ones. We all can fall victim to "a negative self-image." But our children are especially vulnerable. It's reported now that a significant percentage of children go on diets for weight reduction before they are ten. Their awareness of fashion is instilled well before that. If parents don't intervene with a different message, one that is based on the unique goodness and attractiveness of each child, society's rules will prevail.

So that's the first point, to be sure that we as parents look for and affirm the inherent goodness of each child. If we don't, who will? Each of us is quite dependent on the judgment of others to feel good about ourselves. We all know this. And if any of us fail to feel good about ourselves, life can become much more burdensome than it needs to be.

Let's now reflect on the Christian aspect of this issue of judgment. In the Lord's Prayer, we tell God, "thy will be done on earth as it is in heaven." In following God's will, we seek to make life better here. Paul invites us to make the mind of Christ our own.

So how does God judge each of us? God sees us as we are, but focuses on our goodness and moves on from there. When the Samaritan woman encountered Jesus at the well, Jesus did not concentrate on her past life, her many broken relationships, or the fact that she came to the well in the middle of the day, a fact some Scripture scholars say was quite inappropriate. Wells were visited by good women in the early morning. In other words, there was a great deal "wrong" with this woman, and Jesus could have judged her negatively.

Instead, he treated her as a person wanting to do better. He affirmed her in her goodness and encouraged her to do better. Not only that, he pressed her to go and tell others about him. She became a disciple with a mission. No doubt she shocked those who knew her because they had written her off long before. But not Jesus. He wrote her into his plan for the salvation of the world. The power of focusing on goodness can bring about miracles!

If the truth be told, all of us could do with large doses of persons noticing our goodness. We should declare one day a year, no, one day each week as Goodness Affirmation Day. It would probably become our favorite day of the week. We notice and describe the goodness we see in others, especially our children. Maybe our kids would even notice it in us. Wouldn't that be a welcome surprise!

Families could create "goodness charts" for family members and post them on the refrigerator door. We could add goodness accounts to our evening meal prayer. We might shock neighbors and people we work with by mentioning how we've noticed something good about them. As we leave church, we could tell the priest that we found something good in the homily (besides it being brief). We should try to be specific in our judgments and communication. Avoid vague generalities. The more specific and concrete we can be, the more power our words will have.

Goodness always surrounds us. The challenge is to notice it and allow its power to fill us with joy. God created us to be happy. As

C.S. Lewis wrote, we can be "surprised by joy." God created us and judged it to be "very good." Our job as parents is to accept this and to tell others, especially our children.

Prayer

Dear God, you judged your creation as very good. Help us recognize goodness in everyone, especially in our children and in ourselves.

For reflection and discussion

1. When have you been told by others that you were good? Can you describe the effect it had on you?
2. What would you say are the best qualities of your children? Have you ever let them know what you think?
3. Does our Christian faith help or hinder us in our desire to accentuate the good?

HOPE

Overcoming unavoidable fears

May the God of hope fill you with
all joy and peace in believing,
so that you may abound in hope
by the power of the Holy Spirit.
ROMANS 15:13

Fear not. Be not afraid. We find these words and others like them over 200 times in the Bible. It could be called "the standard biblical greeting." When the angel appeared to Mary announcing that she had been chosen to be the mother of the Messiah, God knew exactly how she would react. How anyone would! So the first words she heard from the angel were, "Do not be afraid, Mary, for you have found favor with God." Once that was taken care of, they could move on.

God knows what's in our hearts and how we typically react to the challenges and dangers that come every day into our life. God also knows that excessive fear can blot out our vitality. Fear can be like acid rain. It etches away the joy that might be in us. It destroys our enthusiasm for life. It can rob us of the happiness God intends for us.

Strong feelings of fear even affect our bodies. When we fear, we can feel our chest tightening as stress builds up within. It changes our blood chemistry. No matter what its cause, our bodies "think" that we must prepare for battle. When our ancestors lived in caves, people feared wild animals. When a saber-toothed tiger appeared at the door, an alarm went off signaling that danger was present. Fear levels escalated. The body prepared for defense. The situation called for full attention on the intruder. Tigers can be dangerous.

But suppose there's no tiger. Suppose that instead of wild animals to worry about, we simply fear the future, the unknown or the uncertain. Do we react any differently to these general concerns? Not really. Research about stress shows that our bodies, and our minds as well, constrict when fear overtakes us. Our thinking becomes focused on the object of our fear. Our bodies tense. Our whole being prepares to take on the enemy.

Because of our strong reactions to fear, Jesus invited us to let go of unnecessary fear and anxiety. We pray for this at the Eucharist. We are called to place our trust in God who cares much more about humans than the flowers of the field. Look at them, Jesus said. They're not worried.

Can we understand how fear might affect us as parents? Fear comes with the territory. We fear for the health and well-being of our children. We can fear the uncertainties about their futures as much as our own. As parents, we are saddled with many financial responsibilities, so fear over money matters and jobs can easily escalate. We are also vulnerable to the fears of society around us.

Some fear is necessary. It helps us get going and get busy about caring and working for our families. We need money to live and to provide a good life for those we're responsible for. So I'm not suggesting that it's even possible to be totally fearless. The danger is excessive fear. The kind of fear that generates chronic stress. The kind of fear that brings on a stroke or heart attack in young parents, as well as older ones. The kind of fear that takes over our whole life. That's not good.

The strongest medicine to reduce fear is developing trust. In religious terms, trust implies our belief that whatever the challenges we face, we will survive. We call this placing our hope in God. We trust in God's concern and promised assistance. Our Christian faith becomes real and quite practical as well. We trust that we will not be destroyed. Some of our dreams may not be realized, but deep down, our lives will be good enough. This kind of belief is no small matter. We accept that God is truly on our side, and even more, that God cares for us, especially our children, no matter what!

What grounds our hope goes well beyond an optimism that pushes us along on dark days. Rather, we affirm God's presence and power in our lives, especially when we face trials and difficulties.

I have mentioned already that my wife and I adopted two children who had experienced serious difficulties before they came to us. When the opportunity arose for adopting them, we were nearing our sixtieth birthdays. Because they had once been foster infants under our care, we were told that their previous bonding with us would greatly help them. It was not an easy decision for us. But we were supported by the willingness of our older children to help, as well as by hope and trust in God. We needed it all!

Philosophers and theologians who study the deeper dynamics of religion note that the real power of faith comes to the surface when we reach our limits. When we've exhausted our resources, when there is no more that we can give, we move to a place that might be exactly where God can work with us. We pray for help, God listens. We are not omnipotent. We cannot solve every problem. So we have to let go and trust in divine help.

I remember a time when one of our sons came home from school quite concerned and fearful. He had crossed the line with one of the school bullies and was given a warning that tomorrow was to be his day of reckoning. As I listened to his worries, part of me wanted to protect him, but that may not have been what was best for him or me. That night I prayed that God protect him.

The next day was a very long one for me. I imagined my son with a bloody nose or even worse, lying face down on the sidewalk next to the school. When he returned from school, I noticed right away that he looked much as he did when he departed in the morning. I asked him what had happened with the bully. He offhandedly said that the two of them had talked, and it was cool. I breathed a sigh and silently said a prayer of thanks. I know that it always doesn't end so well, but I don't know what I would have done were it not for the fact that I relied on God's power to help. All parents have these moments.

Prayer

Dear God, with a simple divine word you created the entire universe. Support all of us, especially our children, to walk through life with hope and confidence in your abiding help.

For reflection and discussion

1. Have you ever had to rely on hope or trust in God's help? What were the circumstances? Did your reliance on hope assist you?
2. Can you think of ways our culture prevents us from needing to hope? Is hope a virtue needed only by the weak?
3. How do you usually deal with the fears in your life? Can you name your major fears? A clue for helping you do this is to think about what you most worry about.

INTIMACY

Connecting across the kitchen table

Now that you have purified your souls
by your obedience to the truth
so that you have genuine mutual love,
love one another deeply from the heart.
1 PETER 1:22

Each time our family sat down for the evening meal, we'd play a kind of game called "positives and negatives." The rules were simple. Each night a family member would say grace, and then start the table conversation by mentioning at least one positive experience he or she had that day. Positives were followed by negatives. We proceeded by age, starting with the one whose turn was that night. For many years, my wife's mom lived with us. When it was her turn, about ninety-nine times out of a hundred her "positive" was, "Well, I made it though the day." Our young children found great satisfaction listening to what their grandma would say when it was her turn. Her words were always greeted by howls of laughter. It was as if they could predict her response and they were almost always right. Then she would add that she didn't have any negatives. Another round of chuckles. Through the children's laughter, the family was one.

Our little game insured that at least once a day we all connected through communicating. Even visitors to the table were dragged into the ritual. I can't say that everything important was said. Children, especially when they enter the teen years, seem to keep a few more secrets with each passing day. But something personal was always communicated, and that something was better than nothing. Honest communication is the lifeblood of family life. And when communication happens, intimacy is possible.

The experience of interpersonal intimacy is the passageway to a deeper life. Philosophers like Martin Buber, the great Jewish sage of the last century, would say it's necessary for basic human life. It feeds our desire for a fuller, more intense life. The essence of intimacy is mutual interpersonal revelation. Heart opens to heart.

Genuine communication requires a speaker and a listener. Honest and clear speaking needs open and attentive listening. The better we are at both these activities, the better we will connect with each other. Further, communication can be shallow or deep. Surface communication is about things, numbers, facts. It's like one newspaper talking to another. We exchange information about the weather, the political scene, how our favorite sports team did in their last game.

We go a little deeper when we share how we feel about the facts. For instance, we might feel depressed when our team loses in the last second of their recent game. Or we mention delight because the government is lowering the tax rate. More of who we are comes to light through this kind of telling.

We move even deeper when we communicate about other persons. We might make judgments about certain friends of our children or about the strange habits of Aunt Rose. Talking about how we feel about others reveals something important about ourselves. This is inevitable.

We communicate on the deepest level when we talk about ourselves—our values, beliefs, and feelings. When we also share how we feel about the person we're communicating with at that moment, we enter the sacred realm of intimacy. As our conversation unfolds, the relationship between us surely deepens. Based on mutual sharing, we create the possibility for more fully accepting, valuing, and loving each other. Because there is really no limit to the possibilities of love, communication, and intimacy, these qualities continue to grow throughout our lives together.

Intimate moments fire our sense of being alive and worthwhile. In knowing that we are accepted with all our liabilities and deficiencies, and realizing we are known and loved as we really are, we experience some of the greatest blessings in life.

Our children need affirmation as much as they need nourishing food and clean air. Parents need the same genuine intimacy that can happen between family members, but while the family setting is a safe harbor for this, it can also be one of the most difficult and challenging places for true intimacy to occur.

This dual aspect of family living may appear paradoxical, but it really makes sense. We know one another, and we know that, like the legal system portrayed in the media, anything we say or do can be used against us. In addition, family memories are set in stone. Their half-life extends well beyond old age. So we are sometimes overly careful about what we communicate in the family.

Some family members fear intimate disclosures. Perhaps they suffer from low self-esteem or a fear that, if they were truly known, people would not like them.

Another barrier is that families easily fall into shallow routines of daily living. We imagine that we've heard everything there is to hear. We can coexist rather than commingle our lives. That's why it's good to occasionally step back and almost plan to communicate. We can ask new kinds of questions or bring up a common interest and really talk about it.

Here's some advice for parents of young children that I have found quite helpful. When children are young, we parents sometimes wish they would quiet down. The constant talk about inane TV characters or the funny smell in the neighbor's house can drive a parent crazy. But try to endure and enjoy this more vocal period of their lives because a time will come when they may talk less. Then quite important topics will need airing, but it will be difficult because the regular pattern of communication may no longer exist.

Deep down we all want to be close to others. That's partly because the closer we are to others, the closer we are to God. In fact, all the discussion so far about intimate communication applies directly to our prayer life with God.

Prayer

Dear God, you are always close to us. Awaken us each day to your presence and help us be close to those we meet every day. Help us know you through them.

For reflection and discussion

1. Think about those times when you truly felt close to someone. What was your communication like? What helped it along?
2. Is it really possible for a parent to experience intimacy with a child? What is your own experience of this?
3. How is intimacy a part of our Christian life? What's your reaction to the final point that communication within our families relates to our prayer life?

JUSTICE

Balancing on the backyard seesaw

For the word of the Lord is upright,
and all his work is done in faithfulness.
He loves righteousness and justice;
the earth is full of the steadfast love of the Lord.
PSALM 33:4–5

If you have experienced it, you will remember. You were on one side of the seesaw and another kid, maybe a brother or sister, was on the other. You were stuck at the top. The other person had maneuvered their weight to create a condition of rigidity. "Let me down. Let me down," you cried. Then, in what may not have been a playful move, the person at the bottom got off and suddenly you came crashing down. In the process you learn something about control and how it feels to have it or not.

Let's examine another variation on the seesaw. You and your partner decide to try and balance it. You work together to create the exact amount of weight on either side. You try to place the seesaw in a totally horizontal position. You find that once that's achieved, you have to continue to work on it, making constant minute adjustments, going back and forth in fully cooperative moves. It's demanding, but you discover that the accomplishment of working together is fully worthwhile.

So what does all this have to do with Christian parenting? The seesaw experience provides a wonderful image for understanding something incredible that's going on in our world. Many are now seeking to accomplish one of the greatest and most arduous tasks ever attempted by humankind. What is it? It's a world where full respect and equality exists between everyone!

Gone would be all those rigid systems that enslave one group to another because no one would be thought to be essentially any better than anyone else. We would all stand before God, young and old, male and female, rich and poor, at the same level. We would each possess a full measure of deep human dignity. We are all created in God's image. We all deserve full respect. Perhaps this may sound quite idealistic, maybe even revolutionary, because it is.

The shift toward greater equality has also caught the attention of social historians studying the family. They note that in the last hundred years there's been a noticeable change in family structure based on a greater recognition of the dignity and rights of both women and children. They also suggest that we are witnessing a certain amount of foot-dragging on the part of those who want to retain male superiority.

Our faith is a strong and reliable source for the affirmation of equality. It comes from a rich tradition calling for social justice. We are all called to a ministry seeking justice. It is a most difficult challenge we face as a church, as a nation, and as people sharing Planet Earth at this time. Hopefully, it's better now than it was years ago, but we all know that it can be much better. And one of the key places where the work of this kind of justice is done is within the family.

First of all, the social movement toward affirming the full dignity of each person has made a massive impact on the institution of Christian marriage. It does not take a Ph.D. to know that marriage was traditionally a bastion of male dominance. In many parts of the world, this unfortunate situation still remains. A recent study of land ownership throughout the world concluded that less than one percent of the world's land is held in the name of women.

Married couples can feel they are blazing new trails as they seek full equality within their marriages. Their effort is partly based on the social justice called for in the gospels. While men and women may differ in social roles and in many aspects of their human nature, the differences should not in any way imply a hierarchy. The best marriages are made of two strong individuals, bonded by love and jointly pursuing in equal amount the many tasks enjoined by marriage. They seek to balance the seesaw.

A similar "balancing act" continues when they become parents. Circumstances will vary with each couple, but the challenge of living each day as equals before God and before each other remains. We now use the language of co-parenting. Both mom and dad equally accept the full responsibilities of parenting.

In the relationship between parents and children, the same rule applies. All are equal before God and should be treated as such. That includes the children. Parents are given by God the task of caring for God's precious little ones. At the beginning children are totally dependent on their parents for survival. But this should not lead parents to assume attitudes such as ownership or domination of children. Sometimes we say that parents are entrusted with children. That language captures some of this important notion of equality. Once again, children come to us parents from God. They are sacred gifts of the highest order. They are neither our possessions nor extensions of our personalities. In their own right they are children of God and endowed with the fullest measure of human dignity and value.

When this kind of justice-thinking enters the day-to-day life of families, it creates the need for high-level calculus. It may require new thinking. Children have a voice in family decisions in accord with their abilities. And so do the parents. We're back on the seesaw, trying to balance not only two, but perhaps many more on the apparatus. Talk about complexity! Absolutely.

But think of the potential results. We create a genuine community of persons where each individual is valued. Family responsibilities are dished out equally. As already noted, this will not be easy. We must swim against the stream of eons of tradition. The family stands squarely in the middle of one of the great social movements in human history.

Prayer

Dear God, you live as three, equal in all ways. In creating all of us as equal in your sight, help us so we can know and appreciate the deep equality that joins us.

For reflection and discussion

1. Can you give some examples in your family experience where equality was not practiced? When did this happen?
2. What aspect of our Christian faith teaches us that we are all equal? Are there any aspects that move us toward the opposite conclusion?
3. If we treat our children as equals, does that mean that parental authority goes out the window? What's your thinking about this?

KINDNESS

The glue bonding fragile persons together

And what does the Lord require of you
but to do justice and to love kindness,
and to walk humbly with your God?
MICAH 6:8

Kindness is not often thought of as an important family virtue. Maybe it's because we take it for granted, that is, until you ask a family therapist about the families who come for help. Or before many families are observed as they work their way through the local supermarket. Sometimes ordinary kindness between family members appears to have taken a vacation.

The word "kindness" comes from the same root word as kin, meaning one's relatives. It's an ancient word that might stem from how much family members depended on each other's help for basic survival years ago. Preparing the family meal, which insured that the family didn't starve to death, was the work of many hands. Growing or catching the meal was a momentous task in itself. Preparing it required bowls and utensils, of course, a fire, and often hours of dedicated labor. Fast food was unheard of. All the actions necessary for the meal required complex coordination, with the whole family working together in unison. To accomplish this, they all learned to work together, to adjust to tasks that were sometimes quick and easy and other times terribly arduous. Family members had to be attuned to each other and respectful of what each one did. In other words, they had to be kind to each other.

The question for today is this: Do we still need this virtue for family survival? Should parents work on being kind to their children? And conversely, do children need to learn the attitude and skills of kindness toward their parents? What role does simple kindness play in the daily life of today's stressed and stretched family?

Of course, all family members need to attend to being kind to each other. It eases the tension that so easily arises when people rub shoulders with each other day after day. Family life exposes both the good and the not so good side of our personalities. We especially know each other's weaknesses. We're not like turtles with hard shells protecting us from a harsh and demanding environment. Our coverings are soft and easily wounded by piercing words of complaint or conflict. We can even be hurt by silence or the "cold shoulder" treatment of others. When too few words pass between family members, you can easily conclude that the intensity of family life has been diminished.

Kindness feeds interpersonal sensitivity. I recall coming home from work, and our youngest son, barely able to speak, asked me, "How was your day?" A simple question pouring forth from his kind spirit. All I remember about that incident was that whatever my day had been up to then, it suddenly became a lot better!

Young children learn the skills of polite mannerisms through following parental urgings to say "please" and "thank you." Such gestures can be signs of kindness. What's sometimes lacking is to have these words used within the family. They are not just words for coworkers or strangers at the mall.

We all recognize how painful the bite of critical or negative family words can be. Likewise, we also know the power of a compliment or a well-chosen greeting that brightens the space between parent and child, especially when these are not simply routine expressions. Family words can heal or hurt like no others.

In Paul's first letter to the Corinthians we find that wonderful poetic description of love in chapter thirteen. There we read, right at the beginning, these inspired words, "Love is patient; love is kind." The two qualities of patience and kindness are correlative. They shine on each other drawing forth depth and significance. When we are patient with others, feelings of kindness and gentleness are always there. And when we act kindly toward another, will they not sense our patience with them? The word "patience" comes from the Latin word meaning "to allow." When patient, we allow others to be as they are. We don't force them to change as a prerequisite to our respecting and loving them. We take them as they are. Earlier we quoted Mr. Rogers saying to his young TV viewers, "I like you just the way you are." He embodied kindness, which is one of the reasons that children so loved him.

The Dalai Lama often mentions that his religion is essentially kindness. He sees a direct connection between being kind to all and the attainment of peace both internally and throughout the world. The practice of what he calls "loving kindness" breaks downs the separation between the self and others and allows us to be more fully mindful of each other. We feel more alive and in touch with all that surrounds us.

A story is told of the first meeting between the Dalai Lama and Pope John Paul II. It was a momentous occasion since they were both thought of as great spiritual leaders, although representing very diverse religious traditions. Their conversation could affect many. Before they talked, however, the Dalai Lama suggested that the two men spend the first ten minutes of their meeting in silence while they looked at each other with thoughts of kindness. Given such a beginning to their dialogue, it is doubtful that when they began talking they would debate or argue.

The connection between parenting and kindness becomes clear when we reflect that kindness toward our children creates immediate bonding. Kindness pulls us closer together. It creates a positive mood where understanding and love can deepen.

Kindness is perhaps described as the soft side of love. It creates a safe setting where anything and everything can be more easily aired and discussed. Because family closeness no longer depends on hundreds of acts of sharing work to insure survival, other opportunities are needed to create and sustain loving family ties. How we enter those moments of "hanging out together" will surely influence the results. Starting with and retaining dispositions of mutual kindness may be the best nutrient to grow a healthy and happy family.

Prayer

Dear God of kind love, may we learn to value each other's goodness and treat each other with gentle kindness.

For reflection and discussion

1. Recall moments when you experienced kindness in your own childhood. What were they and how did they influence you?
2. How do you see kindness as part of your Christian life? Does kindness strike you as an expression of strength or weakness?
3. How is kindness compatible with having family rules, strong boundaries, and a firm structure in family life?

LOVE

A song with a thousand variations

"This is my commandment,
that you love one another as I have loved you.
No one has greater love than this,
to lay down one's life for one's friends."
JOHN 15:12–13

Love is to Christian parenting as sun and rain are to flowers. It's needed in order to grow and bloom. The sense of being loved by a parent triggers in a child a mass of desires, hopes, and dreams. The child feels appreciated and valued, gifts of immeasurable importance.

Parental love takes on many shapes as the child develops into being an adult. Every stage of growth is important. Failure to stay in loving contact with the child will be a loss to both the child and the parent. Did you notice that I mentioned parent too? It was very intentional. One of the more interesting insights of those who study human development is that good parenting benefits the parent as well as the child. Speaking as a parent, if I missed something along the way in my own development, I can somewhat redo that period of development as I live through the same stage in my child. Sounds a bit mysterious, doesn't it? But some say it works.

So how might parental love look during some of the primary milestones of growing up? Let's start at the beginning, when parents must dedicate immense time and energy to caring for an infant. On the surface, it may seem that little is going on. But we now know through sophisticated brain monitoring that major building is taking place in the infant's brain and nervous system. The best image I've seen to understand this process is to compare humans to computers.

When children are born, they come into the world with basic hardware. All the wiring and parts are there, but very little is connected. What connects the circuitry of computers is what we call software. That sets up the ability of the computer to, well...compute! What connects the thousands of parts of the infant's brain is the quality of the interaction between infants and others, mostly parents. So one of the ways parents show love to their new baby is to do all those silly things parents do, like making strange sounds, funny faces, and other outlandish acts around the crib. It's all important. It makes the infant think and associate enjoyment with the presence of others. This is also called bonding or attachment, but most of all, it's love. During infancy, parental love means presence.

When an infant begins to explore the world, first by crawling and then by those first wonderful wobbly steps, the parent is close by, encouraging, enticing, and welcoming the child into discovering the great world that God has made for us. Parents are like tour guides who arrange the best trip imaginable through whatever new place is scheduled for that day. During toddlerhood, love means support.

Childhood is twenty-four-hour play time. It can wear down even the most fit of parents. More of the world is visited, like playgrounds and stores. It's a time for new friends in the neighborhood and at school. Sometimes the parent needs to be close at hand and fully visible. Sometimes the parent can hide. I recall once when our two young daughters decided one warm afternoon to search for gold along a stream near our home. Together we walked to where they thought the mother lode was. Once positioned and digging into the eroded hillside, I sort of backed off. This was their moment to find whatever there was to find, all by themselves. I would have been in the way. That's one of the most difficult decisions for parents, when to stay close and when to back off. We must always attend to their safety, even into the teen years. But we can also be overprotective by not allowing them the space to experiment with their abilities. During childhood, love means watching out for danger.

The teen years are very challenging for many parents. Teens have been described as children in adult bodies. Not only do they outgrow their clothes at an alarming rate, but they also take their first steps toward outgrowing their homes and families. They want more independence and freedom. They want to stay out late and to go everywhere because "all the other kids do." These growing pains often create tension and conflict in the family. Suddenly teens think their parents are out of date and out of touch. And parents think their teens are standing at the edge of a dangerous precipice. The problem is exacerbated by the fact that both teens and parents are right, up to a point. During the teen years, love means staying in touch.

Of course, during each of these periods of growing up, love means a lot more. It always includes communication, warmth, and attentiveness. Concern for another, the child, is a major part of the parent's life. More than anything else in human life, parenting requires altruism and sacrifice. Children enlarge the world for parents and take them to places they may not otherwise go. It cannot be said that all these new locations would be ones that parents would freely choose on their own. But God is really everywhere, so in their own way, teens help their parents grow up by providing them a learning opportunity for exploring even more of the world.

God's love for us is not something intended to be abstract or distant. Jesus pointed out how the love of neighbor was wrapped into the love of God. The first place children learn about God loving them is through their experience of being loved by their parents. This is one of the most important truths of Christian faith. Love of God pours into us by being loved by others. That also means that parents are like sacraments, expressions of God's love for children.

We can spend a lifetime trying to grasp the full meaning and power of this reality. Imagine, God using us as bearers of divine love in all our ordinariness, through our strengths and weaknesses, on our good days and not so good ones. We are like walking sacraments or portable tabernacles. In a very real way we are Holy Communion for each other. And we don't even have to leave home to do this. In fact, in so many ways, it's at home, within the family, that this "making present God's love" is done most effectively.

The great nineteenth-century Jesuit poet, Gerard Manley Hopkins, wrote that Christ plays in a thousand places and in a thousand faces not his own. Where are those places? And whose faces are they? They are everywhere but especially with loving parents.

Prayer

Dear God, whose name is Love, help us show your love to our children in all that we do for each other, however small and ordinary our deeds may be.

For reflection and discussion

1. Make your own definition of love. Use your experiences as a basis for your description.
2. List ways that love happens between parents and children. Try to make your examples as earthy and ordinary as you can.
3. In your estimation, what is "the state of love" in the world today? Is it growing or declining? What would you consider truly heroic expressions of love today?

MESS

Sure sign of family vitality

Then they cried to the Lord in their trouble
and he brought them out from their distress;
he made the storm be still,
and the waves of the sea were hushed.
PSALM 107:28–29

"We don't have it all together. We missed the dentist appointment; the kids forgot to do a homework assignment; the dog got sick overnight; the broccoli burned in the bottom of the pan filling the kitchen with an awful smell; we forgot to pay the electric bill; and we might have overdrawn our checking account. And that's what happened yesterday!" Sound familiar? Having kids can be nonstop work with any number of crises right around the corner. There always seems to be plenty of family worry. We long for peace and calm so that we can attend to important things, like connecting with old friends or even enjoying a little uninterrupted prayer time. We may feel like we're losing the race or, perhaps, our sanity.

We all carry within ourselves images of an idealized world. Among those images are a few that picture a kind of family life we might prefer. The house is neat and tidy. Soft music plays in the kitchen as a smiling parent scatters chocolate chip cookie dough in even blobs on a cookie sheet. Sun shines through the window. The kids are quietly playing dominoes on the living room floor. In some families this scene might be real, but it seems that in many families, including my own, it may come only the day after we win the powerball lottery.

Sometimes we include as part of our internal "art museum" images of life supported by the authoritative voice of God. Cleanliness is next to godliness, right? Or is it the other way around? Here's one way some are led to associate God with neatness. We stop by our local parish for a quick visit. The space inside is filled with soft light as the sun shines through the stained glass windows. We soak up the beauty and peacefulness of the place. No one else is there. This is truly God's world, we conclude. The space is saturated with what we imagine as the divine presence. We imbibe the peace and calm, and for a minute, so are we.

But wait. Get a grip on reality. Is that the usual way life is for us parents? Is this the shape of the spiritual life God wants of us? Maybe at times, but what about most of the time? Peace or war?

I like to think about it this way. Jesus loved to meet troubled people. He went out of his way to talk with those whose faces showed worry and whose demeanor suggested pain. He willingly entered the struggles of humankind. There are no gospel stories that begin with Jesus asking people, "How's it going?" and they respond "Just great." Maybe God has a special liking for being in the midst of chaos.

This doesn't mean parental life has to be non-stop, white-knuckle survival. There are good days, and we do well to savor every moment of them. We truly need a few of those days or we'll go crazy. But a lot of the time, there's a list of "to do's" that seems endless. Noise is bouncing off the walls when the kids are home. The kitchen is often a mess, and blessed clutter is scattered in almost every room. Maybe what we need are some images of God and the Christian life that include mess!

Have you ever visited a funeral home? They are not places we enjoy going to for obvious reasons. But notice what they are like.

Aren't they almost always places of order and quiet? And you know why? Dead people are often there.

So what's the point? Lively families, families where the energy of the world is found in abundance, are most likely a bit messy. And that's okay. Perhaps it's even good! So what if you have to occasionally step over a discarded coat? What's the evil when the evening's dishes are stacked up next to the sink? Or what if you forget about the pile of overdue library books in the back seat of the car? When you have a lot coming at you each day, you can't be expected to catch and hold everything.

That's family life, especially when you are caring for little ones. Children are works in progress. Their memories are not yet fully installed. Their view of any long-range anything remains foggy. Plus, wherever life is lived with intensity, there will always be surprises and some rough edges. You cannot plan for a bowl of spaghetti dropped in the middle of the recently cleaned kitchen floor or an accident by Grandma who now lives with us. Uncertainties happen!

We all need to occasionally question our assumptions about the good life, even the spiritual life. We are fed images of order and beauty. When you open the latest issue of one of those home decorating or remodeling magazines, what do you see? Are rooms littered with old newspapers or the morning's used coffee cups? Hardly. Everything is in perfect order. The pictures on the wall are perfectly aligned, all the accessories match, no fingerprints anywhere to be seen. Guess what? No one lives there. At least not at the moment when the picture was taken.

They say children will see on TV almost 200,000 commercials by their eighteenth birthday. They will surely feel their influence. But we adults also view pictures in ads and other places day after day. We are affected, too.

Yet the world that is shown to us has no mess. The world we live in does. In which world do real people live? We can add, where will we find God? In the place of perfection or that other place, our home? The answer is that God flourishes in family mess. That's where real life happens, where bodies touch and sometimes rub each other the wrong way. God created the world in all its splendid diversity. Each one of us is unique, a simple fact that, in itself, makes human relationships quite messy at times.

So maybe a little mess is okay. No, maybe it's really necessary for the great drama of Christian family life to unfold with its many moments of surprise, as when someone finally finds that missing puzzle piece hiding under the living room sofa. After cross-examining every family member, it is decided that it must have gotten there all by itself. In ordinary families, many strange events happen.

Prayer

Dear God, look with favor on our mess. Help us accept our blessed limits. Give us a calm heart amid the many challenges of each day.

For reflection and discussion

1. Is mess compatible or incompatible with the way you think life should be? How do you personally feel about mess?
2. What is your take on the idea that you might not see your family life as spiritual because it's simply messy?
3. It's Saturday morning. You have a choice. Play with the kids or shampoo the spotted living room carpet. How do you decide?

NEGOTIATING

Judging with the wisdom of Solomon

You desire truth in the inward being,
therefore teach me wisdom in my secret heart.
PSALM 51:6

The story of how Solomon came to be known as a wise person is a wonderful family story. Two women came to him requesting that he as king solve a dispute between them. The issue was very serious. Both women claimed to be the mother of the same infant. After some deep thought, Solomon came up with a solution to their dilemma. He concluded that they should simply cut the infant in half and each one would be satisfied. He knew what the true mother would say. She would never allow such a solution, so out of love for her child, she said that the other woman should take the infant. And she did. Recognizing her genuine maternal love, Solomon, of course, gave the infant to the true mother. It was a brilliant solution. How wonderful it would be if we had such wisdom to resolve disagreements and conflicts.

We parents are often put in a bind by the decisions we have to make involving our children. We pray for wisdom and guidance, but we know that we are often left alone with the burden of deciding. As an aside, single parents will say that having to decide on one's own is one of the hardest parts of being a single or lone parent. It's often helpful to talk with another adult. So many times we parents face choices where black and white revolves into a thousand shades of gray. So often there are good reasons to say "yes" and an equal number of good reasons to say "no."

Further complications rise from our own need as parents in balancing what we need to survive and be happy over against responding to the needs of our children. Parents who always do what their children want soon feel victimized. Parents who always do what they want may be overly self-centered. I often recall situations where one of our children would go ballistic while complaining, "Last week you said I could go to the movies and now you say I can't. That's not fair!" In other words, my thinking lacked consistency. My retort, "It's different this week," had no merit for my child. As she sauntered out of the room with a frown, I could hear the disappointment being voiced: "My dad is really stupid."

The art of negotiation or mediation is highly prized in the business world. Disputes between labor and management are endemic to our economic system. Those who do this effectively are well paid and valued. They sense the common ground between both sides. They know the limits of each one's position. They are sensitive to the position, desires, and needs of both parties and can find acceptable compromises.

In the family, however, there is no middle person to orchestrate solutions to disagreements. The PG-13 movie that the thirteen-year-old daughter wants to see with her friends (all of whom can go) calls for the proverbial wisdom of Solomon. If parents stand against the stream, they feel pushed into a corner with other old-fashioned, out-of date, and uncaring parents. It's not easy being a responsible parent these days.

The first point to make is that the effort to decide what we're calling "negotiating with the wisdom of Solomon" is worthwhile and holy in itself. This is always taxing work. Assembling all viewpoints, listing all potential outcomes, respecting the needs and rights of each person—all of this is no easy matter. The struggles of the average family to make the best decision rivals the deliberations of the Supreme Court.

Next, ultimately the judgment of parents must prevail, but this is not simply because parents are bigger (which sometimes they aren't) or that they have God-given authority over their children (which they do, but it's not simple). This may have been the rationale of the way things were done "in the olden days," but it's not that way today—nor should it be.

First, hopefully we parents have acquired more wisdom and experience in dealing with the complex issues facing us day after day. We see the implications and long-range effects that are simply not obvious to the mind of a child or a teen. Parents understand cause and effect. They know how emotions can overwhelm clear thinking. They have a bundle of experience that enlightens their judgment. They may not know everything, but they know quite a bit more than their children do.

Having established the position of parents, it's important not to short-circuit the full process of decision making. No place is more effective in teaching our children how to make good and virtuous decisions than in the family. The members know and respect one another.

The goal is not necessarily to make everyone happy. Rather it's to do the right thing and to call for the kind of action that will benefit everyone the most and, hopefully, will hurt no one. Sometimes compromise is required.

Perhaps you've heard the story of the family where the parents wanted to go on vacation to New York and take in some Broadway shows while the children had their hopes set on Disneyland and the beaches of Southern California. So they compromised, took out the map of the United States, and went to watch the wheat fields of Kansas as they swayed in the wind. That's called a lose/lose arrangement. It's not desirable.

The trick is to find out what's behind people's preferences. What needs are being unmet? What desires are not being honored? Look at the deeper stuff. Sometimes that takes patience and very open listening, especially on the parents' part. At times kids don't really know what they want. They hear a commercial on TV and suddenly they "need" what's advertised. On other occasions, their friends have a video game or CD or they want to see a certain movie. Guess what? Your child wants the same thing. While we parents might want to dismiss this kind of influence, we might recall that we too can be moved by similar forces.

A rich learning opportunity is often connected with making good family decisions. The whole spectrum of values and history of morality can be brought to the table. Once when our youngest son was five, he announced at the dinner table that he no longer believed in God. Fortunately I remained silent while our other children proceeded to offer their own version of the five proofs for the existence of God, found in the writings of Thomas Aquinas. They were not aware of their sources, but the level of philosophical discourse from our children was a marvel to behold. Besides, they were quite willing to take on their little brother, whatever the reason. Family discussions and debates can be real learning moments, for both parents and children. What's more important is the discussion, not the resolution. In fact, some things are worthy of eternal discussion.

Prayer

Dear God of wisdom and understanding, give us the light we need to make good decisions for our family. Help us all listen to each other and value the wisdom that comes from each member of our family.

For reflection and discussion

1. Recall a recent family discussion. Evaluate how all the parties participated. Was everyone given a voice?
2. When do you feel you successfully resolved a family discussion or debate? What did you do that helped? Do you recall a time when you didn't do well? What was that like?
3. Why is it important for parents to have the last word? What is it about the structure of the family that recommends there be a clear boundary between parents and children?

OPENNESS

Thriving in a waning world

"I came that they may have life, and have it abundantly."
JOHN 10:10

Deep down, at the deepest part of parenting, resides the gift of life. This gift comes directly from God with each new person created in God's image. In God's inscrutable yet trustworthy wisdom each person comes into being through an act of human love and openness between a man and a woman. It's best (all would agree in principle) that they be joined in marital love. They will open their hearts and provide a setting for their child where the truth and joy of human life will be learned, including knowledge of the divine origin of all life. This lesson is best learned through knowing and feeling the love that exists between the dad, the mom, and the child.

We have been reflecting on the many facets of Christian parenthood, especially by focusing on the sacred vocation to assist God in assisting our young to attain full Christian maturity. We have discussed the many needs of children right from the first moment of their earthly lives. But we have also kept an eye on the personal and spiritual life of parents. There's an old Latin phrase that goes like this: *Nemo dat quod non habet.* (No one can give what they do not already have.) When applied to our life as parents, this means that we need to take care of ourselves so we have something to give.

Giving life to a child is more than procreation. It includes everything that follows in the child's life.

Have you ever heard the rumor, quite common I'm told, that parenting is a drag? It is like a giant vacuum cleaner, sucking life from the parent. Whether it happens financially, psychologically, or some other way, the depletion is rather constant. First there's loss of sleep, then loss of time, then loss of money, and finally loss of energy. (Some parents also lose their hair.) Not a happy picture for parents. The parent gives and the child takes. That seems the idea. But does it have to be true in all cases? Can this loss of so much be turned around so that it's gain—for everyone?

In the world of physics, one of the first laws is called the Law of Entropy. In brief, it stipulates that a closed system of matter and energy inevitably wears down. Energy decreases as it's used up until there's none left. When applied to human life, we might compare it to the way we feel after a very trying day. We're totally worn out. Our energy level is near zero. The battery reads dead. All we can think about is sleep.

Returning to our experience of parenting, is this law of entropy a necessary and inevitable feature of our lives? Is parenting a process of depletion and certain loss? Some would think so. But do we have to agree? Can our parenting in general (we all have a few bad days!) stimulate our own growth, enrichment, and fulfillment? I hope so, but I also recognize that it does not happen automatically. I would assume that God intends this as well.

So much of our experience of life depends on the attitude and beliefs we bring to the table. There is no doubt that for some parents the effort, the expense, and the worry that comes with parenting drains their vitality and spirit. But for others, it's not that way. They find ways to love their children and enjoy their presence. They don't use a calculator to measure expenses. They feel that parenting is an honor and privilege. They want to share all that they have received with the ones given to them by God. And they know that it's important to be open to God and to their children every day. The body survives when all the arteries and veins remain open to the flow of life-giving blood. In a similar way parents who "stay open at all hours" can remain vital both for their children and themselves.

Here are some habits that will help life flow in us and through us.

- Acknowledge the newness of each day. Begin afresh. Learn something new every day. Seek new perspectives on old problems.
- Keep your mind alert. Read something enriching as often as possible. Visit libraries and museums. If you can, take a course to broaden your perspectives.
- Engage in long conversations with friends and family. Focus on positives. Surprise someone by a visit or phone call.
- Meet new friends and keep old friendships fresh. Relationships are alive and need regular nourishment.
- Take leisurely walks alone or with others. Notice the world. Go outside on a starlit night. Stop and count the stars. You might want to read a recent book on astronomy. Many are now available, filled with amazing explanations of the universe.
- Talk with your children (and all children) whenever you can. Listen. Ask questions. Encourage them to learn all they can. Smile upon them.
- Do at least one enjoyable activity just for yourself each day. (This is a big one!)
- At least once a week try to do one new thing that you've never done before. (That's pretty big, too.)

Doing some of these things will help us to be more aware and mindful of the life surging within us. Positive moments stimulate us into our own reflections on being alive. They can prompt us to more readily ask why we are alive. Or are we persons of generosity?

Do we believe that we are basically here to share with others all that we have received?

These are deep and challenging questions. They cut to the center of life. They also open us to the deepest part of ourselves, where we meet not only our true self, but also the presence of the living God! Open yourself for the life God has promised in abundance.

Prayer

Dear God of abundant might, keep us alive and smooth the road we travel as parents. Give refreshment to our spirits and bodies as we care for your beloved children.

For reflection and discussion

1. List some activities that are life-giving for you. What have you done in the last week that added to your enthusiasm for living?
2. Some people energize us while others don't. Be sure you connect with those who do. Can you name two or three people who seem able to enrich your life? How much contact do you have with each of them?
3. What's your view on the big philosophical question: Is our world becoming more alive or wearing out? In general, where do you stand in response to this fundamental question in your own life? Does your view influence in any way how you live?

Healing heartburn before it arrives

The fruit of the Spirit is love, joy, peace, patience, kindness, generosity, faithfulness, gentleness, and self-control.
GALATIANS 5:22–23

We had occasion to briefly reflect on patience earlier when we recalled how Paul listed it with kindness as one of the first characteristics of Christian love. Parenting calls us to be patient with our children in the many ways they drive us to need that virtue. Many of us have had to say the prayer, "Lord, give me patience. The kids are driving me nuts!"

Patience is the pressure release valve in all of us. Picture this. It's just a few minutes before we're supposed to leave for church. Our youngest child is nowhere to be seen. I check his room. Guess what? He's fallen back into dreamland. The pressure instantly builds up inside me. I shake him, maybe a little too hard. "Get up. We have to leave in five minutes." He slowly opens his eyes. I toss his clothes on the bed. I am furious and my stress level is at the danger point. He rises and I go to the garage to start the car. Then it hits me. God is everywhere. Our parish is but one of the places God hangs out. God is with our son right now as he tries to figure out what's front and back on the shirt he's putting on. In fact, God is right here with me in the car as it warms up before facing the winter cold. Why fret? Relax. Enjoy the moment. Be patient.

Developing this new attitude of patience before departing for Sunday Mass would be good. I benefited more than my son. I need patience. All parents do. To be an effective and loving parent, we first have to be patient with ourselves!

Many of us parent our children by deciding what we think is best for them. Sometimes we operate from our own narrowness, as when we attempt to impose on them our preconceived hopes and dreams. We all do it. Often, we're hardly aware of this. But such an approach can be ill-advised, even dangerous. Experts in the field often say that we parent as we were parented. That, of course, is not always the best way to address this deeply complex, relational task. For instance, I recall a family expert once saying that spanking children was fine. He was spanked as a child and he claimed that he turned out fine. End of discussion? I hope not.

In fact, our own efforts at parenting help us undo some of the unhealthy and even harmful patterns of parenting that may have existed in our families for longer than anyone can remember. Part of good living is constant awareness of why we do what we do. It's called being reflective or using the intellect that God gave us. Parents need to do this.

The process by which we seek to undo bad family habits is called family differentiation. In cleaning up our parent act, we become healthier and more helpful by examining the influences that have affected our own growing up. After identifying them, we can dispense with those that possibly were injurious and move ahead, less fettered by harmful tendencies of our past.

A personal example. I grew up in a family strongly influenced by racial and ethnic prejudice. In my early twenties I recognized the presence of this harmful attitude in myself. I have spent much of my adult life trying to eradicate it. Another area of great anxiety in my family had to do with money, mostly its absence. Again, another lifelong struggle for me.

No one can deny how important it is to be self-conscious and critical so we can be more faithful to being our true self. Translated into parenting language, we all want what's best for our children. Sometimes we want this too much. So we often become impatient, and that's where we need to focus. Parents know those special areas that test their patience. After a while, wisdom may enlighten us that the problem may be ourselves!

What are your hot buttons? When do you find the demon of impatience rise from deep inside? You may want your children to be at the top of their class, just as years ago you wanted the same for yourself. You may hope that they will be good in sports or have a lot of wonderful friends, just as you wanted when you were their age.

When we fail to achieve our parental goals in our children, we may become impatient. What makes it all the more difficult to recognize this is that our hopes for our children are wrapped in love. But this love can have too much of ourselves in it. It can be possessive love.

Like many Christians, I have struggled with the biblical passage about Jesus and what he said on one occasion about his family relationships. It recently came to me that this story may help me to be more patient as a parent. Recall the episode. Jesus was surrounded by a large group. Someone noticed that his mother along with other family members had arrived and stood at the edge of the crowd. They told Jesus that his family was there. But instead of stopping everything and greeting his family, Jesus appeared to ignore them and responded with apparently biting words, "My mother and my brothers are those who hear the word of God and do it" (Luke 8:21). Was this an intentional put-down of his own family? Was he being disrespectful? What was really going on?

My own view is that Jesus was saying that there is one primary relationship we all share: our relationship to God. This relationship is deeper than the connection between mother and son, husband and wife, or brothers and sisters to each other. God comes first; family flows from that.

Jesus' words were not a put-down of Mary, his mother. He was comparing her relationship and all the rest of our human relationships to our relationship with the One who is the ultimate source of our life.

Doesn't this kind of faith in God assist us in parenting our children in a helpful, more patient manner? I believe it does. It gives us a bit of healthy distance from them. They are not our absolute possessions. They are, first of all, God's children, and God's intent for them is primary. Maybe that's enough reason for us to lighten up and be more patient.

Prayer

Dear God, lighten my worries by helping me to be more patient with those I live with, including myself!

For reflection and discussion

1. In which situations is your patience most tried by your children? Are certain areas more volatile than others?
2. How do you try to parent differently from the way you were parented? What were the best qualities of your parents? What about the not-so-good ones? Can you identify these?
3. What do you see as the greatest benefits from being a more patient parent?

QUIET

Creating deep moments

Let your adornment be the inner self
with the lasting beauty of a gentle and quiet spirit.
1 PETER 3:4

It is right after Christmas. The reports are being aired on TV about the most popular Christmas gifts this year. The winner was a highly portable, miniature electronic device that can store more than a thousand pieces of music. The message is clear. Always be tuned in. Your music is available wherever you are. You never need to exist in the curse of silence.

Just before Christmas, our family was about half way on a 900-mile drive to visit my wife's parents who were then retired in sunny Florida. Our family van was moving slowly southward through Georgia. Very slowly. It seemed that half the population of the United States and Canada was seeking a winter break on some Florida beach. Out the window, we saw red clay everywhere.

"All right, it's quiet time," my wife announced over the clamor in the back seats. We had five children under ten. The clock had just hit the top of the hour. Every forty-five minutes, we observed fifteen minutes of delightful silence. That was our custom. And no giggling either. This break in the action was the only way we felt that we could arrive at our destination with some semblance of sanity.

A few days before, I had picked up some beach reading, a new edition of Henry David Thoreau's *Walden Pond.* It was a book I had read in college but was much too immature back then to understand its powerful message. For those unfamiliar with it, it is an account of the two years Thoreau spent alone on the banks of a small pond, just outside Concord, Massachusetts. It was the "noisy" time around 1845. His book endorsed the value of quiet reflection on one's life. He believed that we all need quiet moments to connect with the deeper dimension of our lives. His book's message is timeless. He wrote, "I went to the woods because I wished to live deliberately, to front only the essential facts of life, and to see if I could now learn what it had to teach, and not, when I came to die, discover that I had not lived.…I wanted to live deep and suck the marrow of life."

Like so many who attempt to touch the depths of their own lives, he warned against the terrible cost imposed on those who failed to live with deep-rooted awareness and understanding. In the same piece, he wrote a sentence that has haunted many: "The mass of men lead lives of quiet desperation." How a person might determine this, I don't know, but I don't believe that it was originally penned as a judgment of others, but as a wake-up call to whoever might read his words. Again, a timeless challenge.

Back to "quiet time" in the van. I'm sure the need for parental quiet is obvious, but it's something our children need, too. The development of an interior life, a place inside where we entertain silence and reflection, can only be nurtured by creating quiet on the outside. To me, one of the misfortunes of today's youth culture is a seeming absence of silence. I applaud teachers who set aside quiet time in the classroom, and parents who declare an occasional moratorium on TV watching and listening to the constant clatter of an audio player or computer.

Our culture is very much externally driven. Sounds fill our malls, elevators, and even our phones when we are put on hold. Many people can't seem to drive their cars without the blare of a stereo system accompanying them along the miles. Similar stimulation can fill our homes with music piped into every room or with TVs omnipresent programs. The latest place for TV watching? The bathroom!

With all this noise entering the space surrounding us, our minds can easily descend to overload, our senses become dulled, and our thoughts turn into mush. An unacknowledged cost marks this attention given to outside stimuli. We no longer think or imagine or pray. Our thought processes turn to gruel. We can't find within us the quiet where that part of us that is the most important, our interior life, can live!

Like Thoreau, who lived in a much slower-paced time, we all need moments of quiet.

In quiet we digest our moments and deepen our feelings. We grow in awareness of ourselves and each precious moment that passes by. In solitude and quiescence, we more easily see the deeper part of others. As I mentioned earlier, the story is told of the first visit between the Dalai Lama and Pope John Paul II. Before they talked with each other, the Dalai Lama requested that they first gaze at each other in silence with thoughts of loving kindness. For ten minutes! I suspect that once they began conversing, they got deep right away.

It is reported than many men find their sanctuaries of quiet reflection behind the wheel. On the other hand, women report finding peace within, especially while soaking in the bathtub. Holy places need not look like Gothic cathedrals.

Given the always hectic pace of contemporary parental life, I believe we all need quiet moments when we can awaken our deeper self. Don't make the false conclusion that time taken alone necessarily takes you away from those you love. Ironically, quiet thoughts about the ones you love serve to deepen your ties with them. You notice their wonderful qualities that you might take for granted or have not even noticed! When we are alone, we can feel closer to them, feeling their pull in their absence.

The same can be said about our awareness of God. We need quiet to feel the elusive and airy presence of the divine Spirit. God is always there, which creates the challenge of being aware of that presence. God is there a millimeter under the surface of everything but always under it. Never obvious, never in our face.

Enriched and deepened by quiet time, we parents can more easily appreciate the gift of life in our children. We can more easily handle the inevitable difficulties they bring. Quiet can dispel anxiousness and allow us to find more effective approaches to daily problems. I have read that there's a quiet room at the headquarters of the McDonald's fast food empire with only a bed and skylight. Hamburger executives are encouraged to spend time there when thinking about what's next for the company. Years ago, when faced with the prospect of a growing number of seniors in our population, they were asked to think about how they might attract this potential market. One day, an epiphany happened in the quiet room. The message received? Breakfast! So was born the Egg McMuffin. We all need quiet moments for new thoughts to grow within us.

Prayer

Dear God, help us break through the noise of our lives to find what's most precious: your presence and an awareness of the gifts you give us each day.

For reflection and discussion

1. What's your favorite time and place for quiet? Do you find time to do this regularly?
2. How do you slow down the pace of your life? Do you have a set way of doing this? Do you have a favorite way of praying in quiet?
3. How do you encourage the growth of an interior life in your children? Do you see the absence of this as a problem today?

RECONCILING

Mending broken hearts

"So when you are offering your gift at the altar,
if you remember that your brother or sister has something
against you,
leave your gift there before the altar and go,
first be reconciled to your brother or sister,
and then come and offer your gift."
MATTHEW 5:23–24

We all know about home repairs. Household appliances can stop working at any moment, often right before a big feast. Cars are not built to last forever. They often break down right before the big family vacation trip. But what about family relationships? Do they last forever? Do they occasionally need maintenance and repair?

The answer to all of the above is obvious. Almost everything needs repair at some time. Close relationships, like those in a marriage or in a family, are some of the most difficult to put together after connections have been broken. In this reflection we'll talk about how to mend a broken heart or a severed connection between parents and children.

Point number one: It's never easy. People are not things. You need more than super glue to mend severed ties. The bad news is that this task can be very challenging. The good news is that we can almost always do it.

One of the most well-known stories in the gospels is that of the prodigal son. It's a family story. The younger son wanted his inheritance early. In other words, he couldn't wait until his dad died, or worse, he wanted his father dead. He took the money and ran away to a distant land. In a short time, he blew his full inheritance on immoral living. Having exhausted his money, the son decided to reinstate himself, not in his original position as son, but as a hired hand on his father's ranch. Logic seemed to require a drop in status.

The father saw him coming home. In those days, sons ran to fathers, not the reverse. But, as Jesus told it, the father was overcome by his love. He ran to embrace his wayward son. Everything went into reverse. It was a new day. The past was forgotten. Love won! Reconciliation was accomplished. The party began. New rules were set for life and relationships in God's kingdom.

One day not too long ago, the silence between my son and me was killing me. I said something I didn't mean to say. The wall went up, the wall of silence. I knew it had to come down. He was my son. He was a teenage "test pilot." He had flown where he shouldn't have, and too fast. They caught him going twenty miles over the limit and well past curfew. Our relationship hardened like the surface of a pond hit by an arctic front. By the grace of God, I walked into the kitchen where he was sitting, nursing a glass of milk. "Want to go to Dairy Queen? My treat. I'm sorry I shouted at you."

"Me too. But I deserved it. Can I get whatever I want?"

"Absolutely. Even if it requires a second mortgage. Do we have any coupons?"

It's so easy to create a wall between us, but it takes twice the effort to knock it down. Barriers can be constructed between mom and dad, kids and parents. Egos are hurt, and the children run for cover, often as far away as they can. Anger is a great, quick-setting cement.

Also, like cement, anger hardens through time. The longer the wall stands, the harder it is to get it to fall.

Those responsible for building walls often present a grim face. They hurt, but they allow themselves to feel self-righteous. They are one-up, in the power position. Reconciliation often has to begin with humility. So, we swallow hard and make the first move. Sometimes that move includes a request for forgiveness. Yes, this can be quite difficult.

Long-term anger is like carrying a boulder on our back. It wears us down. It's hard to fly through life with unresolved anger. Family squabbles and disagreement swallow family vitality. No one talks and no one looks the other in the eye. When a family has anger on or beneath the surface, it's like chronic constipation. You don't talk about it, but it hurts.

It's never too late to mend broken relationships. Hospice workers often tell stories where the last wish of a dying person involves family reconciliation. We don't want to leave this life unconnected with those closest to us. Family alienation is sad beyond words.

One of the hardest parts of family reconciliation involves making the first move. Who breaks the silence? Who swallows their pride? Our tendency toward self-righteousness is rarely more alive than when there's a need to mend brokenness in the family.

Because parents are older, more experienced, and hopefully more mature as Christians, parents should make the first move when there's a rift with their children. Children can be more dominated by fear than parents are. That means that parents may be more able to initiate and literally create a new world, like the father in the story of the prodigal son.

Further, we might recall Jesus' teaching that in all matters of relational connection, God always, yes, always makes the first move. God loves us first. Those who say that we must say we're sorry before God forgives us have it backwards. God's grace is always the spark that ignites the fire.

The church has wonderful contemporary examples of leaders who took the initial step toward forgiveness. John Paul II met with his would-be assassin, and Cardinal Joseph Bernardin of Chicago invited the young man who falsely accused him of sexual misconduct. Their purpose was the same: reconciliation.

One of the most basic of all religious questions is whether the world is biased toward good or evil. Jesus came to settle that issue. It definitely leans toward hope and resolution of conflict. As we all know, evil and conflict happen but God does not intend them to have the last word. Reconciliation is the dessert of all full-course meals.

Prayer

Dear God of mercy and forgiveness, you are always the first to forgive. Give us parents some of your spirit that brings us all back together.

For reflection and discussion

1. How do you know when reconciliation has happened in your family? What are the signs of peace?
2. Why do you think that reconciliation is so important in our lives? What are the costs of unreconciled situations?
3. Can you recall an instance when you took the first step toward reconciliation? How did it go? Would you do it again?

SMILING

Seeking happiness beyond family photos

God saw everything that he had made,
and indeed, it was very good.
GENESIS 1:31

I am a major problem to my family because of family pictures. Ask any of our kids and they will tell you, "My dad always closes his eyes when we take family pictures. He ruins them."

In my defense I have argued that I am smiling so hard that my larger-than-average side cheeks push upward and close my eyes. No one has yet accepted my explanation. I have been told more than once that I need to deal with my problem because family pictures are an important part of the family memories. Who wants to remember their dad as someone who never opened his eyes?

In photographs taken during the "Dark Ages" of a hundred or more years ago, most people look grim and determined. They look as if they've just been told a really bad joke. No one smiles. Life seemed to require a serious effort just to survive.

In contrast, observe today's family pictures, like the ones received in Christmas notes. Looking at the smiling faces, one might wonder whether the whole family had just learned they had won the latest Powerball lottery. So the inevitable question is this: Are we happier today than our ancestors were? After all, the camera doesn't lie. Well, if we know anything about the history of photography, we know part of the answer. Back in the days of flash powder and large, box-sized cameras, the shutter speed was so slow, that in order to capture a sharp picture of the family, everyone was told to stand very still for a longer time. It was easier to do that with a serious look on one's face. Smiles tend to dance around some, so they didn't smile.

I don't know why we smile at cameras these days. However, we do most of the time, regardless of our feelings at that moment. People seem to develop a camera look, which is seen no matter when or where the picture is taken. Sometimes it appears a little forced. Fake smiles are not what I'm advocating here. They need to be real and come from deep inside.

Mental health professionals claim that smiling is very good for us. It releases the flow of healthy chemicals that can benefit circulation and breathing. Genuine smiles, they say, are also connected with the functioning of our immune system. In other words, for better health, it's good to smile.

But sometimes to smile is not easy. Weighed down by worries and the usual problems parents face, we are more likely to frown or look worried than smile. That's okay. Honesty both inside and outside is important.

One of the best pieces of advice I ever received as a parent was the simple admonition: Lighten up. Take it easy. Be considerate of those you are responsible for. Give them room to grow. This was not an invitation to irresponsibility, but for some balance, and a reminder about life in general. As Christians, we know that God has worked hard to create a world beneficial for our well-being. Yes, life is challenging and difficult at times, but taking everything together, we're supposed to accept the gospel as good news. The victory has been won. Trust in God's care. Don't try to do it all yourself. In other words, lighten up.

We live in an era when the advice of mental health experts fills our magazine pages and talk shows with personal programs for perfection. We can sometimes be drowned in parental shoulds and should nots. Do this and don't do that. Monitor your child's diet, free time, friends, television viewing, educational growth, athletic performance, and so forth. I'm not advocating the much-maligned permissive approach to child-rearing, but I wonder whether we sometimes can overdo our parenting role.

So here's the test. Can you let the warming rays of your smile fall regularly upon your children? When they remember you years from now, what will the look on your face be that they recall? Grimace or gladness? Smirk or smile? Are we more like drill sergeants or demanding coaches or teachers? Can we sit back, enjoy the simple presence of our kids, and smile?

Smiles are very important. If the eyes are the windows to the soul, the smile is its door. A simple smile welcomes others into our life. It proclaims that something good is happening within us. There's warmth from the fire that burns in our soul. A genuine smile can melt another's icy heart.

Smiles brighten the world, too. A child breaks into a spontaneous smile when mom walks into the room. After a teen passes the worrisome algebra exam, a smile comes out, and the whole house lights up. When Grandma in the nursing home sees her grandchildren at the door of her room, she smiles from ear to ear and causes the whole building to take on an unmistakable glow. Genuine smiles are, without a doubt, utterly contagious.

I recall those many moments when, as a new parent, I tried to coax a smile from our infant children. The antics I performed, the funny looks I attempted are well forgotten. Under these circumstances, we often resort to unmitigated craziness. Eventually it happens. From somewhere deep inside the newborn, signals are sent, nerves carry a new message, muscles twinge into a shape never before made, and a smile springs forth on the infant's face. Talk about lighting up the world! As a parent, the first smile of a child is never forgotten. And we know, too, that with that smile, everything, yes, absolutely everything has changed. Through that smile, the child announces, "I'm here and I am happy I'm with you."

One of the best gifts we give to one another is a smile. I have occasionally wondered whether God smiles on us, or more to the point, whether God smiles on me. Once I was flying across country late at night. When I fly, I sometimes think about spiritual matters. Maybe it's the altitude. Maybe it's the miracle of moving between distant places with grace and ease. Anyway, as I sat in the quiet plane, I began to wonder how God looks upon at me. Suddenly I imagined God smiling on me. That's a moment I shall never forget.

Prayer

Dear God, let us feel your smile upon us. Help us find our own smiling spirit that we can use to lighten the day for everyone, especially for our children.

For reflection and discussion

1. Has this reflection on smiling made any sense to you? Has the case for smiling been overstated? Or is smiling one of those things we can never get enough of?
2. Is smiling something we can control or is it something that just happens?
3. How does smiling relate to our spiritual life? Does it have a role? Do we need to smile more in church?

TIME

Creating moments that will last

"The kingdom of heaven is like treasure hidden in a field,
which someone found and hid:
then in his joy he goes and sells all that he has
and buys that field."
MATTHEW 13:44

There is lot's of advice out there about financial investment. Money is big in our world. Most people are looking for ways to have more. Of course, we all know, sometimes too late, that there is no such thing as a sure thing—life is more complicated than that—and the world of finance is a good example of this uncertainty. The world is filled with people who were led to invest in one thing or another only to bail out with empty pockets for their efforts. I know. I have been among their number. Nevertheless, investing remains a good idea.

Years ago, I learned that one of the best investments lies in creating positive family memories. Unlike most steps in the financial world, the results are guaranteed. The advice to invest in family helped to decide the direction we should take when the way was unclear.

Many examples come to mind. It's Saturday morning. I could clean the garage or take the kids for a hike. We could look at new cars or take a family vacation to a national park nearby. In many of these situations, both options were good. What's the better thing to do? I'm suggesting that we should give more weight to choices that create good family memories. This is especially important when children are young. Any good moments we experience with our family last a lifetime, perhaps even beyond.

Another simple example. I grew up in Indiana, a state known for being a little nuts about basketball. I bought into the sport as a youngster, developed a fairly decent jump shot, but ended my official career just before the varsity level in high school. I lacked the abilities needed for the next level. Still, I stayed active in the sport, and over the years have enjoyed many moments of exhilaration that come from "draining" an impossible shot in a game of "horse" with our four sons.

So when we have the opportunity to do so over the years, we like to shoot hoops. Sometimes our effort turns into a game among us, sometimes not. A passer-by might think that we were merely practicing our shots. Wrong. We are connecting. Talking. Horsing around. We are creating extra-special family moments. Shooting hoops is a treasured family ritual. We've done it before, and we hope to do it again.

I would add that our shooting around, along with similar family activities, makes for genuine play. We may keep score in "Twenty-one," also called "Long and short," but half an hour later no one remembers who won. Play is that wonderful human activity when all the attention is on the moment. Goodness flows from "doing what's being done" and not from results. Philosophers call this "living in the moment." What's important is that such play is not just for the moment. It creates lifelong memories. We carry these moments inside us as priceless treasures. We recall them during our final years.

Current studies of family life list time as a most precious commodity. We want more family time in an already overcrowded life. A few years ago, the notion of quality time entered our discussions. It referred to those moments in a day when we were more present and alive, happier, more involved. It was judged important to plan our life to insure the possibility of quality time.

Today the concept has been adjusted by simply seeking quantity family time. A one-minute approach simply falls short when it comes to family life. Parents and children can too easily float apart, given the many demands on time for all family members. How often do we read that our lives today are overscheduled? There is little if any free time. We multitask to get things done. The average workweek is at an all-time high. We all must deal with the frustration, and maybe even some anger, that comes with the realization that we can't do it all. We try time management. We become very time conscious, mostly driven by the idea that we need more. These days you can even purchase electronic, highly sophisticated day-timers for children!

When engaged in demanding physical exercise, we need warm-up time and cool-down time. Something similar happens around family events. Time with family can be terrifically intense and emotionally demanding, and may take considerable energy to do well. Yes, family time can be pleasantly relaxing, but sometimes it takes a lot of effort to reach that point. So enriching family time may require some large chunks of time. The question all parents face is whether it's worth it.

Like so many parents, I have had to face the time problem. I have learned to say "no" not only to requests from others, but even to myself. I make lists of "things to do" and then face the world of reality at the end of the day, or month, or year with too many items left undone.

Yet, the challenge remains: What about time with our children? Where do their needs (which are also partly my own) fit into the calculations needed for survival? How does my Christian faith enter this discussion? What's becoming clearer is that how we spend our time is one of the more important moral issues we face. Jesus said that where your heart is, there you will find your treasure. He was referring to the values he proclaimed as coming from God. So what were those values? Were not most of them about being with others and helping them? Especially with our neighbor. And who is my neighbor? Who is nearest to me?

We are given the gift of time. With that gift comes responsibility. As parents, there is no simple formula for deciding how much time we need to set aside to create family memories.

Granted, the benefits of sharing time with our family are often intangible. I don't get a dollar for every walk I take with my wife. We don't get points by sharing food with our families at dinner time. My personal GNP is not affected by how many long shots I hit when shooting hoops with my sons. But deep down, we know. For family is created, built, and blessed by the moments we share. They always count.

Prayer

Dear God, you have created the days and the nights, the years and the seconds. Help us use these treasured gifts with wisdom and purpose.

For reflection and discussion

1. How do you deal with time in your own life? Are you a planner or are you more like a responder to needs as they arise? What do you see as benefits of both approaches?
2. Look back on your own growing-up years. Can you take any lessons from what you now remember as important times? Is it valid to compare then with now, or has everything changed? What do you consider as timeless values?
3. What use of time most nourishes your family?

UNDERSTANDING

Getting at the whole truth

My mouth shall speak wisdom;
the meditation of my heart shall be understanding.
PSALM 49:3

I enjoy traveling to places where they speak a language I know only slightly. It gives me a deeper appreciation of the marvel of communication. I struggle to order an egg for breakfast. The waiter listens to me and perhaps thinks I am asking for a chicken. We go back and forth. Maybe we draw a picture. Finally another miracle happens. The waiter understands what I am thinking. I wait to see if I will be surprised at what's served.

Interpersonal communication is one of the greatest achievements imaginable. We form sounds and, when they are heard, they have meaning for another person. We express the subtleties of our thought through language. We seek to create mutual understanding. We come to know each other as unique persons as well as persons sharing the same life through language.

The family is like a factory for language. Think of the work involved in getting an infant to first say mama or dada. Less effort is needed to climb Mt. Everest! We recognize how essential it is, especially in the first few years of life, but it remains so throughout life.

Just before my dad died, I tried to converse with him. He was only partially conscious. When he was a child, his family mostly spoke Lithuanian, the language of his parents. Now because of the mysterious ways of the mind, he had reverted back to that language. I myself knew very few words in Lithuanian. I did know how to say, "good bye" and "thank you," and I said them. He smiled. It was our last exchange. Blessed are those families where communication flows freely. They will know all the more about each other. One cannot overemphasize the value of such knowledge.

I recall studies about young children who were asked what their parents did, besides being parents. Where did they work? What did they do? It was amazing to discover that many children didn't know much at all about their parents' work life. In some instances this knowledge gap motivated the practice where children now accompany one or both parents to work one day a year. This is a fine idea. Our appreciation of each other is directly related to our knowledge about each other's everyday life.

A few years back, some beneficial research was published about the different ways women and men communicate. Apparently our brains work in slightly different manners. My eyes were opened by this research. I never knew these differences existed, but having been informed, I can understand and appreciate women much better than before.

For instance, it was reported that women use language to form connections. Men use language to inform and to solve problems. This difference in the use of language influences the flow of words and information between the genders. Women use language to find agreement and similarities. Men tend to use language mainly to discover differences and disagreements. These differences need to be recognized if we are to fully understand each other, or as I titled this chapter, if we are to know the whole truth about each other. In other words, communication is much more than words. It involves style, context, and intention.

This brings us to the vital topic of listening and interpretation. Any presentation about communication includes a word or two about listening. Listening well is a skill we all need to learn. So many distractions are present both outside and inside us at any moment. We easily fall into focusing on what's next, instead of on the present. When this happens, significant messages can be missed. It's as though we listen with only one ear.

Communication is partly verbal and partly body language. Our tone of voice adds texture. Our feelings can be sensed. How we talk is as important as what we say. Sometimes there's a heavy silence between family members. That, too, can convey a crucial meaning.

One of my friends is a family therapist. He uses a wonderful technique to help married couples, as well as parents and children, to communicate with each other more effectively. The sessions are awkward at first, but they pay huge dividends in the long run.

For example, a husband and wife are seeking help. First, the wife speaks and the husband listens. She tells her side of things. She tries to be as thorough in her telling as she can. Then it's the husband's turn, but before he can talk about his side of whatever the issue might be, he has to first describe in his own words exactly what the wife has said. Until he can do so to her satisfaction, he cannot talk about his views. After that the communication process begins again as the husband speaks to the wife. It's like the old saying: It's not what we say; it's what the other person hears.

Communication is often compromised by the limitation of time, which we discussed in the last chapter. At times families almost have to schedule time to talk. Here's where we need extra sensitivity to the introverts and quiet ones in the family. Think of the family as a power grid. Energy flows from the more powerful to those with less power. Families can often be divided into those members who are active and those who are more passive. Respect and attention given to the quieter ones may take extra effort. Just because people are not communicative does not mean that they have nothing important to say.

A word is needed here about the significance of understanding each other as unique persons, especially in the family. Our minds like to stereotype, label, and generalize. We seek shortcuts in knowing others. We all too easily paint each other's portraits with broad strokes rather than with the fine lines of distinctiveness. Families can categorize each other, for example, "He's the wild one," or "She's the smart student in the family." Such generalizing violates the richness in each of us. If the family does this, how much more easily does this happen in society?

Because we come to know our personalities partly through the way others view us, think of the personal loss we experience when we accept without critical thought the impression others have of us. We all deserve much more. Our families are the best place to help us know ourselves. Families form persons, what it means to be a person, not things or images. The mass media are fully adept at reducing a person to an image. Because of our familiarity with such reductionism, we may follow the same pattern of behavior.

The family should be the place not only where our name is known (the old description of the *Cheers* bar in Boston), but also the place where our unique gifts and our distinctive and wonderful personhood is known, brought forward, and praised.

Prayer

Dear God, you created the universe with a word and speak to us words of love. Open our ears, hearts, and minds to the wonderful words said in our family.

For reflection and discussion

1. What do you consider to be the strengths of your family's communication? What might be its weaknesses?
2. Why is good family communication so challenging? Do you think it's easy or difficult to communicate honesty in the family?
3. How do you feel when you perceive you have been truly understood? Why is that important?

VARIETY

Spicing everyday life with adventure

Now there are varieties of gifts, but the same Spirit;
and there are varieties of services, but the same Lord;
and there are varieties of activities,
but it is the same God who activates all of them in everyone.
1 CORINTHIANS 12:4–6

Most of us have heard the phrase "Variety is the spice of life." This also describes God's way of creating. Look at the abundance of variety in nature. Thousands and thousands of species. We've heard that no two snowflakes or tree leaves are exactly the same. New research into the universe shows us stars and planetary systems, each one quite unique. A moon has been seen for the first time around Saturn. It looks like a potato! Certainly no two people are the same either. But here, we're not concerned about similarities or differences of things or people, but how we live and whether we might find ways of being more vibrant human beings. Let's look at the deeper meaning about variety being a spice for living and explore how this might help us be better persons and parents.

I want to focus here not so much on our children, but on ourselves, on our own well-being. Taking good care of ourselves, of course, will spill over into how we parent. It's a win/win equation. Relaxed and vibrant parents always do a better job. Enough can't be said about how we parents develop and stay healthy, especially through the years of active and quite time-consuming parenting.

During the past decade or so, a great deal of research has been focused on how to live a longer, healthier life. Eat the right foods, get plenty of physical exercise, avoid stress whenever possible—we've doubtless read about and hopefully applied these life-enhancing practices. What's clear is that most of this advice comes from the medical profession and is directed to our physical well-being. We might move to a broader consideration of well-being and reflect on how we can enhance our lives on the emotional and spiritual level.

For starters, consider what's being learned from research on the vital elderly, those who are still living with gusto into their later years. If something works for them, it should be good for us, too, whether we're a young parent or a grandparent. While these active seniors may be feeling some of the inevitable aches and pains of aging, they remain active and involved with life. The question for us is, what do they do to retain that spark of life we all desire, both now and later on?

A sampling of their responses includes these recommendations: Don't get stuck in a rut. Beware of mindless routine. Keep your mind alert. Ask questions. Learn something new every day. Get outside. Visit new places. Make new friends. Do you get the spirit of all this? It appears that one of the best ways to survive at any age is to seek newness and be open to a variety of experiences because it is especially through the encounter with the new that the fire inside us remains burning.

Like all living things, our minds need nourishment as much as the rest of us. Again, this is true throughout our lives. Many of us already know this, and we are truly lifelong learners. Years ago public libraries and museums were like mausoleums. They were quiet and mostly empty. Today this has dramatically changed. Public places of learning and exploration are filled with young families, active middle-agers, and vital seniors. The same can be said about our parks and other places of recreation. Vitality and variety are valued, and people are insuring that their lives include a full measure of the action. More and more parishes, too, are involving families in intergenerational faith formation sessions and in parish activities.

One of the dangers for parents is that they wrap their whole lives around their children. They only "go out" when accompanying their children to a game or a performance. They tend to put their own development on hold "until the kids leave." That's not a good idea. We all need a daily dose of inspiration and newness. Otherwise, we atrophy inside, and that's not good for any of us.

Experiencing life-giving variety may seem a bit abstract. I like to translate this value into times for connecting with something or someone new. Try developing a habit of asking yourself at the end of the day, "What's new?" Hopefully, you'll be able to name something specific, something exciting, and perhaps even a little wild. We can also ask ourselves, what's pushing us to new limits? New vistas? New thoughts and feelings? Don't forget to note any new discoveries or awareness of ourselves.

We have already reflected on the scarcity of time and the pressures we face in parenting children who appear to be growing up in a world quite different from the one we knew when we were their age. The direction offered here may seem to be a luxury that we can't afford. Nevertheless, the investment we make in our own growth will translate directly into the quality of our parenting. We will have more to think about and more to communicate with our children. And we might even learn something from them, too. This doesn't happen automatically, but unless the door to our inner self is open, no one can enter. Showing that we are open to new things to learn may be enough to create much deeper parent-child encounters, and some real give-and-take conversations. You can begin by asking your child or teen about their favorite music. Believe me, you will then enter a world of great mystery.

Parenting is a calling in the service of life. Yet life is a whole lot of things. The family has been likened to a living body, each part connected with and passing on life to the other parts. Here we are emphasizing the importance of parents being more fully alive. Every day offers us an opportunity for great adventure, but if we sit around waiting for it to happen, it won't. Remaining active and interested is the key. To give life to others requires that we have received it, or better, are taking it in, minute by minute. One of the best approaches to living fully is to be always seeking new adventures. That's why variety is important. It's both a means of remaining vital and a test as to whether we are on track instead of in the rut of safe, yet lifeless routine.

Prayer

Dear God of wondrous imagination, pour into us the richness of your creation. Astonish us with surprises that will bring us wonder and delight in your amazing world.

For reflection and discussion

1. Can you name a new experience you had during the last week? If not, go back a month or more. Think about the value of that experience.
2. Being more fully alive is part of the Christian life. How do you practice this in your life? What brings you the most vitality these days?
3. How have your children been a source of life for you? Think of specific times when you could almost feel a jolt of energy entering because of an experience or a moment with your child.

WISHING

Desiring the best for everyone

If you abide in me,
and my words abide in you,
ask for whatever you wish,
and it will be done for you.
JOHN 15:7

Sometimes a song is stuck in our heads and we simply cannot shake it. It follows us, like an overly friendly dog, all through our day. When the mind rests, the song still plays. It can be painful, like elevator music.

I have carried a song with me for as long as I remember. I blame Walt Disney because it was on the soundtrack of one of the first movies I ever saw. The song begins, "When you wish upon a star." Many of us will be able to fill in the next lines along with the melody. I was probably all of six when I first heard it as I watched *Pinocchio* at the local theater. I still like the song, but I don't like how it crowds me as background music on my daily walk.

Part of the song's attraction, I suspect, is that its message has almost universal appeal. We're all "star-wishers" at heart. Life is never quite enough at any given moment. We hunger for more. So we wish for good things to happen in our lives. When they do, we give thanks. We also wish for good things for those closest to us.

How sad to learn that some people have given up on wishing, especially if they are children. They no longer expect tomorrow to be better than today. They don't look for good to triumph or for the world to become a more peaceful place. We call people like this cynics. The word has an interesting history. It's a Greek word related to their word for dog. It was also associated with a philosophical sect known for their pessimistic attitude. They were hypercritical, always seeking to find fault or imperfection in others. Cynics tend to be complainers, then and now. They seem to be without hope. When given the chance, they try to take the air out of everyone's balloon.

It should be obvious why parents ought to be people with strong wishes. They should also try to instill a wishful disposition in their children. High on any parent's wish list would be that good things come to their children. Nothing lights the face of a parent like the success of their children. So part of good parenting is creating wishful children. Who wants cynical kids? If they can't be hopeful about this wonderful adventure of life, who can?

I used to think that children were essentially self-centered. That was their nature. So we would expect that their wishes would be mostly for themselves, such as things to ask from Santa for Christmas. But sometimes we are surprised by their altruism.

Like other families, we celebrate the birthdays of our children with great fanfare and jubilation. The highpoint of the day is the special moment of blowing out the candles on the birthday cake. While recently going through a shoebox of family pictures, I noticed that we seem to have an unusually large number of photos of our children blowing out candles. It is one of those important Kodak moments.

One year, our youngest son, who must have been about five, attempted to generate a hurricane level wind inside himself because, as we all know, if you can extinguish the candles with one blow, you get your wish. We heard a Whoosh! followed by total darkness. At five, we can be assured of success. "So what did you wish for?" one of his mischievous brothers asked. His question, no doubt, arose from his desire to block the wish from coming true. Older kids knew that if you disclosed your wish publicly, the game was over. This fact would be revealed to his little brother immediately after he had shared his wish. As I listened in, I fully expected to hear the usual, and quite age-appropriate, wish for a gift such as a new bike or an electronic game.

His response almost knocked me to the floor. "I wished that Dad would find the job he is looking for." This was one of those parent moments that I have never forgotten, especially when as a teen, he...well, that's another story.

This little episode also showed that family wishes can be contagious. My wish became his. Our son knew that my wife and I were quite concerned because dark clouds hovered over my job, and I was looking for new employment. Our anxiety had touched our young son, too. This is a classical example of how the family is a living system.

One of the greatest powers families possess is that of generating family-based hopes, desires, and wishes among its members. Sometimes what's wished for may benefit the whole family. Sometimes the family may wish for something for just one of its members. It makes no difference. It's the wishing spirit that is so crucial.

Further, wishes should not stop at the door but should extend outward to the whole world. Our wishes are a good indicator of the state of our heart. Exemplary families are not insular but participate and contribute to the future of the whole world.

There's a simple self-test of whether our desires have attained their proper largess. Think about your wishes. What are they about and whom do they include? Certainly our wishes should begin "close to home." But they must be larger and include the stranger, our sisters and brothers in Christ, whom we are called to acknowledge and love.

The great Swiss theologian, Karl Barth, said that the Christian home must have both doors and windows. Doors to welcome those who need the warmth of family love and the concern of good Christians, and windows to see God's great world outside our homes. One of the greatest "sins" of Christians has always been narrowness. This failure includes not only what we do to harm our neighbor, but also what good we don't do that we might have done.

Be a parent whose wishes extend further than your means. Have a generous heart. Wish upon all the billions of stars up there to the One who created them all, by making one wish for our unending happiness.

Prayer

Dear God of great power, teach us to reach for the stars and wish for all that you have created for us. May our hearts expand to the ends of the universe and beyond.

For reflection and discussion

1. Do you consider yourself a person with great wishes? What are the "top ten" wishes in your life or list at least the top three?
2. How does the church encourage us to be people with great wishes? Or in your experience does it work in the opposite direction by throwing cold water on the fires of big wishes?
3. How do you encourage your children to have strong and generous wishes and desires for themselves?

XENOPHOBIA

Overcoming fear with hospitality

Rejoice in hope,
be patient in suffering,
persevere in prayer.
Contribute to the needs of the saints;
extend hospitality to strangers.
ROMANS 12:12–13

In creating a guide for Christian parents that follows the alphabet, finding helpful ideas under the letter "X" offers a special challenge. Nevertheless, when discussing and responding to the challenges and complexities of parenting these days, such a difficulty is minor when compared with how to send the right message to a slightly rebellious teen or an easily distracted toddler.

When I opened my dictionary to this letter, the number of options were limited. But when I saw the word "xenophobia," I knew my search was over. This is a perfect word to describe an attitude that can suffocate the family and limit good parenting. The word means "fear of strangers" or "fear of what's judged different." The root word is Greek, *xenos*, which means stranger or outsider.

Overcoming the tendency to be afraid or prejudiced against persons not like us is essential not only in family life, but critically needed for the survival of our planet. We too easily label anyone different from ourselves as dangerous or as our enemy.

Fear is perhaps the most powerful of human emotions. It's directly tied to our desire for survival. Fear was created by God to alert us that danger may lurk in the shadows. When fear totally dominates our lives, we fall into a state of paranoia, which can mean—according to the origin of this concept—"thinking outside the mind." We allow our emotions to dominate us and blind us to reality.

Families can become paranoid. They lock their doors and windows. They put high walls around their homes. They barricade themselves against the outside world. We noted earlier that families need to have a permeable skin, like any living cell. With non-permeable boundaries, we may block what is harmful, but we also fail to connect with what might nourish us.

Dangers are real, especially those that might hurt our children. Much is said these days about ways in which the Internet can be a huge source of harm for the young. We have been alerted to the ways sexual predators use computer communication to reach the unsuspecting and the vulnerable. We know that we shouldn't fear everything, but informed caution is very necessary for caring parents.

So each of us stands watch over our families as we seek to find the best way to live and grow in these challenging times. If we fear everything, we'll never leave home and that's not healthy for anyone. We might be tempted not even to get out of bed!

Some parents (or grandparents) will remember famous actors such as John Wayne, Loretta Young, or Jimmy Stewart in classic films that often embodied many of the values that are part of our nation's heritage. In some ways these movies may have oversimplified things, but they still connected with our lives. In their stories, we enjoyed the easy separation of "good guys" from the "bad ones." We cheered the arrival of the good guys who would save the day.

One of my favorite scenes was in the popular Westerns and usually took place at the local watering hole with a few of the old faithful characters lounging at the bar. At the key moment a "stranger" would saunter in. Eyes immediately riveted on him with apprehension and alarm. This could spell trouble. Hands were lowered to their six-shooters, just in case. Strangers in that milieu always symbolized danger. Anyone unknown to the locals had to be carefully watched.

The air was tense. After what seemed an eternal walk up to the bar, the stranger muttered to the bartender, "Whiskey!" Suddenly, the tension eased as if a gust of fresh air blew into the dusty room. The stranger drank what the others drank. Slowly the silence was broken by someone asking, "Where ya headin', mister?" Or "You ain't from these parts, are ya?" In other words, let's collect some data on this fellow so we know whether we can accept him into our town. Conversation might suggest more commonalities than the same drink. If it was revealed that the stranger was different, fear returned. After all, you can't trust strangers, especially if they are armed.

What does this side trip into the Old West have to do with family life? Plenty. It raises a whole series of important questions like these. How does your family accept differences? Does family acceptance demand full conformity to all family customs and ways of thinking? Not a few families break apart because of differences, especially between parents and children.

One of the important virtues of a Christian home is that of hospitality. A welcome mat is laid at the front door. This spirit symbolizes God's openness to everyone, friend or stranger.

Human growth and the process of reaching maturity include being open to the new, the untried, and the different. At first, much of life appears strange, and therefore, a little dangerous. But we seek to overcome these feelings to learn more about God's expansive world and those who share it with us.

We once had a neighbor whose young boy was afraid of getting wet or dirty. Perhaps this was also his parents' fear. I observed how he would carefully negotiate his way around the neighborhood, especially after it rained. Something in me was uncomfortable with the idea of little boys who were afraid to dirty their hands or feet. One day, right after a spring rain, he came running over to our place. Maybe it was the aroma of freshly baked cookies that drew him. In his excitement, however, he failed to notice a rather large mud puddle in our driveway. Down he went, face first. I was sitting on our front steps and could see the horror arise in his startled face. There was only one thing for me to do. Join him in the fun! So I did. Sometimes craziness assails us, and we act a little out of character. It can be good for us to do so. In the distance I could see his mom frantically heading our way. I didn't think she was coming for a cookie.

Prayer

Dear God, you love everyone deeply. Open our family to the wonders of all peoples. Remove from us all unreasonable fear of danger. Help us embrace life's abundance.

For reflection and discussion

1. We all know that today's society can be dangerous. Many homes have elaborate security systems. How do you view this situation, and how does it affect the way you parent your children?
2. How is the virtue of hospitality lived out in your family? Is it something that you intentionally foster? How is hospitality a dimension of a vibrant Christian spirituality?
3. As a parent, how do you teach your children about the hazards of daily life? How do you encourage a healthy curiosity in them? How do you introduce your children to new situations that might have a dangerous side to them?

YES

Expressing crazy affirmation

For in [Christ] every one of God's promises is a "Yes." For this reason it is through him that we say the "Amen," to the glory of God.

2 CORINTHIANS 1:20

At its deepest level, religious faith is a yes to human existence and a yes to the spiritual journey that each person undertakes. Faith in God is like the acceptance that Mary gave to the angel who brought her news of God's plan for her. She willingly went along. In Latin her "yes" is *fiat*, which means, "Yes, let it be, let it happen, I accept what God offers."

Every affirmative response we make in the face of life's challenges can be thought of as an echo of God's initial yes at the dawn of creation. God's love energized all the good that was, is, and will be. That's a weighty thought but one we are capable of taking in. By appreciating the importance of affirmation, as a repeat of God's creative first word, we will be encouraged to do more of it. Sometimes we respond with affirmation because it's obviously the most reasonable and practical thing to do. But there will be times when we are invited to do so in the face of great mystery and uncertainty. That's when we go the extra mile. As parents we often do this sort of thing. We can be accused of what's been called crazy love, a response to our children that only a parent would make.

The basic word of family life is "yes." Much has been made of Pope John Paul II's culture of life. In such a culture, human life is appreciated, valued, and understood as coming directly from God. God is the author of life. God establishes the purpose of life. The dignity inherent in each person comes as a direct, unmerited gift from God. In God's wisdom, the family is the best setting for life to begin, develop, and reach its fullest potential. We know that this admirable goal is not always achieved, yet the ideal remains.

In families, a parental yes should be heard as often as possible. But is it? Toddlers are often known for voicing the opposite. Experts in child development say that language formation comes through imitation of what's most commonly heard. In fact, some claim that children won't use a word until they have heard it a thousand times. So much for the yes!

As a parent observer of myself and others, I find that many of us have some bias against saying yes. As I reflect on my own responses to requests from my children over the years, I find I've been slightly programmed toward saying no, especially when money is involved. I'm not proud of this admission, but I recognize it as true.

So I would certainly not be in the camp of those who state that we should never say no to our children. Nos are very important when the issue involves danger or risk to our children. "No, don't put that screwdriver into the electric outlet" or "No, you cannot go to a party when the parents are not home" are necessary directives. Children sometimes fail to consider short- or long-term effects of a particular action. A prudent use of no is just as essential in family life as a generous use of yes.

Let's step back and take a very broad look at how we humans develop. We do best when we are affirmed in our choices. A word of support or encouragement goes a long way to bring out our maximum effort. Coaches of athletic teams know this. Good teachers do also. Often a parent's yes results in great accomplishments by these daughters and sons. In the poignant stage play *I Never Sang for My Father*, the grown son desperately hungers for the slightest expression of affirmation and approval from his father. We occasionally hear about a condition called "father hunger," which describes an unfulfilled desire on the part of children for their father's blessing.

Wives and husbands never grow tired of hearing a yes from each other, whether it be the response for a request to take out the garbage or a positive response to the vital questions, such as, "Do you still love me?"

The TV figure Fred Rogers of "Mr. Rogers" fame had a great influence on the young children of America when he visited them in their homes. While his TV program was not exactly exciting, his message was both clear and, for some, deeply needed: "I like you just the way you are." A full expression of affirmation. He felt that children cannot hear that message too often.

Further, a parental yes carries much more weight or value than a similar response from a stranger. When parents affirm a child, they do so with full awareness of all the weaknesses and shortcomings a child may possess. Their yes verges on that miraculous reality we call unconditional love, the kind of love we all most yearn for.

A resounding yes to life and yes to the Creator of life is at the basis of the vocation of Christian parents. This vocation does not receive enough public acknowledgment in the church. Since parenting does not hold the same type of formal position in the church's organization, as, for example, the priesthood or religious life, it is more often than not taken for granted. Further, few married saints have been canonized. So if the exalted role of parents is to be praised, it will be up to parents to make it so.

As families we must give Christian affirmation to ourselves and each other. Maybe we need to create a feastday just for parents. Right at the end of the year, the Catholic Church celebrates "Holy Family Sunday." That might be a good time to affirm the importance of Christian parenting. However, the placement of that feast may not be the best, since it is sandwiched between the great celebration of Christmas and New Year's Day. Christian families are often pretty worn out after Christmas.

So here's another proposal: Decide on a day to celebrate your life as a parent. Have an extra dessert or something that affirms you in what may be the most important role on the planet.

Prayer

Dear God, you affirm us with each breath we take. Help us appreciate ourselves and our children. Teach us to say a holy yes to our children whenever it's best.

For reflection and discussion

1. Can you recall a time when you as a parent vacillated between a yes and a no? Think of when you decided on yes. Do you have any good memories of that time?
2. What do you think about an image of God that makes God into a YES God? How might that influence your prayer life? Or even your day-to-day struggle to survive?
3. What might the church do to affirm the vocation of parenting?

EST

Flavoring family life with joy

The wilderness and the dry land shall be glad,
the desert shall rejoice and blossom;
like the crocus it shall blossom abundantly,
and rejoice with joy and singing.
ISAIAH 35:1

Parenting is a full-time job. Parents never really take a vacation, nor are their work hours limited to a forty-hour week. The pay is minimal, and the demands can be extraordinary. An argument can be made that those of us who do this work are a little nuts. It is not surprising that we can become worn down on occasion. Nevertheless, I conclude our reflections on Christian parenting with a call not only to stay the course, but to do it with zest.

We have been created to experience the joy of God. To wish and work for joy may sound odd to those who view religion and family mostly as serious matters. But the God of love has created us for life in abundance. Not in the financial sense but in a much deeper way. In fact, joy is part of our Christian birthright. Sounds a bit crazy, doesn't it?

I recall seeing a TV program on a food channel where the chef of the day was describing the secret of good cooking. "It's all in the seasoning. Good spices enhance the natural flavors. If you know how to spice, you'll be a master chef." While I'm not particularly interested in becoming a great chef, I do like that person's approach as a metaphor for good living. Without spice, our lives can become dull and tasteless. If we don't parent with zest, we may miss out on part of life's greatest adventures.

The great saints of history were all examples of zest-filled lives. God's Spirit blew through their lives. They occasionally disturbed the status quo. They saw each day as a special challenge to "renew the face of the earth." They were persons of fire and nerve, never resting until the work of God, as they saw it, was done.

May we Christian parents be like that. Let us carry within us tons of enthusiasm for our vocation as parents, as persons who generously share our lives with God's precious little ones. Enthusiasm literally means "God's Spirit living within us." It comes from two Greek words, *en* and *theos*. When we observe someone acting with enthusiasm, we can rightly conclude that part of their energy comes from God. The same is true for energy's cousin, zest. If you meet someone along life's road with an apparent zest for living, take off your shoes. You are on holy ground.

Asian religions teach that conscious breathing is an important spiritual practice. Slowly breathing in and out with full awareness brings us into a deeper sense of being alive. Breathing rejuvenates our bodies moment by moment. But it can also be a rich symbolic activity that signifies we are truly alive. Zest is a great indicator that we are alive—with an exclamation point!

While it's been said that a major part of life is spent just showing up (as it is), we also do well to throw ourselves into each moment with zest, just as God did with the creation of the universe. Or as the father did in the story of the Prodigal Son.

In the book of Genesis, movement toward life began with God's breath (the word also means spirit) blowing over the waters of the deep. With something of God's own being mixed into the pot, exciting, zestful things began to happen. And here's something else to think about, a kind of secret concerning what's going on right now. God is still there stirring the pot, especially in our families. That's why Jesus said that life in God's kingdom has already begun. Sure, much more lies ahead, but we're already in the game. The clock is ticking.

Perhaps you are familiar with the following piece of advice that has been attributed to Saint Ignatius, the founder of the Society of Jesus, commonly known as the Jesuits. He was quite intent on finding God's presence in everything. He gave his advice when approaching matters dealing with the interface between God's grace and our response. Pray as if everything depended on God and work as if everything depended on you. Welcome to the world of mystery and complexity.

True religious language is often filled with paradox, and the words of Ignatius are no exception. So I conclude our conversation about Christian parenting with some ways I have found to keep zest on the front burner.

First, keep your life zestful by trying new things every day. We are creatures of habit. We know what happens when we leave something in the refrigerator for too long. Keep your life fresh and interesting. Once one of our teenage children bluntly requested that I stay in the background when her friends came over. Curiously, I asked her why. She said that I was too unpredictable. I might embarrass her. I secretly took her view of me as a great compliment. One never knows when a flash of zest might appear.

Next, be open to spontaneous celebrations. Many of us have lost the art of celebration. We fast more easily than feast. Yes, we have our Super Bowl gatherings and birthday parties, but are they really celebrations of life? Or are they "just another thing we have to do?" To truly celebrate means to let go. We enter a new sense of time as we dive into the moment. Work becomes play and life becomes a joy. Of course, we can't live that way all the time, but what about an occasional moment when we give ourselves permission to really enjoy life? Parents need those moments to balance the hard times when we worry, with good reason, about the future for our kids or the future of humankind as a whole. Without moments of zest, we fail our children and ourselves, for that's not the way the God of love planned it.

Prayer

Dear God, great cook of the feast of life, remind us to celebrate with zest the many moments of our life. Lighten our spirits so that we can sing and dance wildly.

For reflection and discussion

1. How do you keep zest as part of your life? How do you create moments of celebration?
2. Is zest for living part of your spiritual life? What's lacking in your life right now that could be a source of joy for you?
3. Zest is different for different people. For some it's wild celebrations. For others, it's a quiet stroll in the park. How do you recharge your parental batteries? How do you feel the presence of God's Spirit in your parenting?